Diagonal (or On-Point) Set

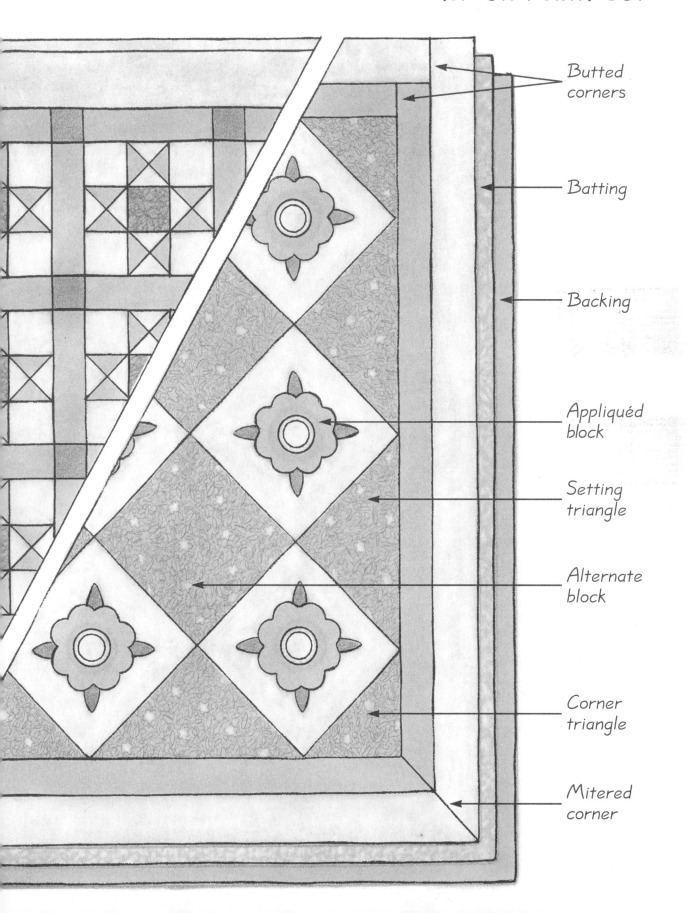

Butted corners

Batting

Backing

Appliquéd block

Setting triangle

Alternate block

Corner triangle

Mitered corner

Rodale's Successful Quilting Library®
Choosing Quilting Designs

Jane Townswick
Editor

RODALE

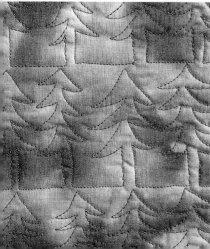

WE **INSPIRE** AND **ENABLE** PEOPLE TO IMPROVE
THEIR LIVES AND THE WORLD AROUND THEM

The writers and editors who compiled this book have tried to make all of the contents as accurate and as correct as possible. Illustrations, photographs, and text have all been carefully checked and cross-checked. However, due to the variability of personal skill, tools, materials, and so on, neither the writers nor Rodale Inc. assumes any responsibility for any injuries suffered or for damages or other losses incurred that result from the material presented herein. All instructions should be carefully studied and clearly understood before beginning any project.

Printed in the United States of America on acid-free ∞ , recycled ♻ paper

We're always happy to hear from you.

For questions or comments concerning the editorial content of this book, please write to:

Rodale Inc.
Book Readers' Service
33 East Minor Street
Emmaus, PA 18098

Look for other Rodale books wherever books are sold. Or call us at (800) 848-4735.

For more information about Rodale and the books and magazines we publish, visit our World Wide Web site at:
www.rodale.com

On the cover: Detail, Great Grandma Goebel's
Red & Green Appliqué Quilt,
by Elsie May Campbell
On these pages: Sixteen Baskets of Mud,
by Diane Gaudynski
On the Contents pages: Canterbury Tales,
by Hari Walner

Book Producer: Eleanor Levie,
Craft Services, LLC
Art Director: Lisa J. F. Palmer
Editor: Jane Townswick
Writers and Samplemakers:
Elsie May Campbell, Joe Cunningham,
Judy Doenias, Diane Gaudynski,
Myrah Brown Green, Laura Heine,
Mary Saltsman Parker, Linda Pool,
Judy Roche, Diane Rode Schneck,
Anita Shackelford, Ami Simms,
Debra Wagner
Photographer: John P. Hamel
Illustrator: Mario Ferro
Copy Editors: Erana Bumbardatore,
Nancy N. Bailey
Indexer: Nan N. Badgett
Hand Model: Melanie Sheridan
Baby Model: Miranda Sheridan

Rodale Inc.
Editorial Manager, Rodale's Successful
Quilting Library: Ellen Pahl
Studio Manager: Leslie M. Keefe
Manufacturing Manager: Eileen Bauder
Manufacturing Coordinator: Patrick T. Smith
Series Designer: Sue Gettlin

**Library of Congress
Cataloging-in-Publication Data**

Choosing quilting designs / Jane
Townswick, editor.
p.   cm. — (Rodale's successful
quilting library)
Includes index.
ISBN 1–57954–331–6 hardcover
1. Patchwork. 2. Quilting. I. Townswick,
Jane. II. Series.
TT835 .C465 2001
746.46—dc21   00–051735

Distributed in the book trade
by St. Martin's Press

2 4 6 8 10 9 7 5 3 1 hardcover

Contents

Introduction

If you enjoy making quilts (as I do), sooner or later you are bound to encounter the words "Quilt as desired" in the instructions for a project you want to make. At first glance, this phrase seems simple enough; the imperative form of the word "quilt" simply means that it is now time to stitch the three layers of your quilt sandwich together, either by hand or by machine. If you are already an experienced quilter, this is an easy task. And if you are trying your hand at quilting for the first time, there are many great books, magazines, and classes that can teach you the technical side of hand or machine quilting easily and successfully.

It's the *second* half of that phrase—the "as desired" part—that can be tricky. I remember how I reacted the first time I read those words as a beginning quilter: "I don't have the faintest idea how I desire to quilt this project." I didn't even know where to start looking for quilting design ideas, so I decided on simple outline quilting ¼ inch away from the seams of the patchwork pattern in my quilt. It was an acceptable choice, certainly a traditional one, and maybe even an effective look for a small pieced quilt. In any case, outline quilting was the only option I could think of at the time, so it was all I knew to "desire."

It took many years for me to gain enough experience to be able to "desire" a variety of quilting styles to enhance the quilts I made. If there had been a book like this one available when I made my first quilts, I would have enjoyed the opportunity to choose from a wide array of creative quilting options. As I edited this volume, the innovative ideas in each chapter kept increasing my awareness of the unlimited possibilities that exist all around us for gorgeous, new quilting designs.

As an appliqué designer, I enjoy developing interesting motifs and images for my quilts. I gained a lot from the "Great Inspirations" chapter on page 42, which offers creative ways to use elements from greeting cards, home decor, and architectural details for creating quilting designs. I know I'm going to enjoy using what I learned in "Let the Fabric Tell You" (page 16), as well. I am already "hearing" some of my favorite prints "talking" to me about mirror images, symmetry, asymmetry, and border repetitions. And I love the freedom that the "Simple Shapes, Super Effects!" chapter offers for drafting interesting quilting designs from circles, squares, and ellipses. (See page 52 for those techniques.)

The next time I'm ready to do some machine quilting, I'll head for the chapters called "Doodling Around" (page 60) and "Fun, Fresh, and Free-Motion" (page 64), which contain whimsical ways to embellish quilts with a wide selection of messages, random designs, and interesting threads. And when time is of the essence, I know that I can count on finding great ways to get a quilt quilted fast with the hand-tying and machine-tacking methods, buttons, ribbons, and other options in "Finish It Fast" (page 102). In fact, I can't

think of any quilting need that isn't covered in these pages!

After you've enjoyed exploring the new horizons in quilting designs throughout the book, check out the gallery of gorgeous masterpieces made by quilt artists from all over America in "Strategies from the Experts" on page 106. Each of these talented quiltmakers shares his or her personal approach and quilting philosophies. Their discussions are filled with innovative quilting ideas that will surely make you want to start creating your own inventive and original quilting designs right away!

Great information flows through every page of this book—and if you're like me, you'll want to keep it close at hand, for easy access whenever you see the words, "Quilt as desired."

Happy stitching!

Jane Townswick

Jane Townswick
Editor

20 Top Tips for Marking *Quilting Designs*

1 Test *any* marking pen or pencil you wish to use on every single piece of fabric in your quilt top that you might use the marking tool on. Make sure that the tool marks a line you can see easily and that will come out completely when you've finished quilting.

2 For dark fabrics or busy prints, mark quilting designs with "dustless" white chalk—the same chalk used on blackboards in schools. Use with quilting stencils to mark highly defined lines that are easy to quilt and that brush away easily after you finish stitching.

3 If you plan to use water-soluble markers, be sure to double-rinse all of your quilt fabrics after you prewash them to remove any possible detergent residue. The pigment in these markers can react with chemicals in your laundry detergent, causing your marks to turn brown and become permanent.

4 Water-soluble markers come in blue, purple, and even white, with fine or medium tips. When using a water-soluble marker, mark with a very light touch. Pushing down too hard on the pen can flatten the tip, making the lines fuzzy. Keep several washout marking pens on hand, and switch between them so they last longer.

5 Don't try using a plant mister to remove marks made by water-soluble markers! That will wick the ink into the batting and make it reappear later. Instead, wait until you finish quilting, and soak the quilt in clean, cold water in the washing machine for an hour or two to remove the markings. Use the spin cycle to remove the excess water, and dry the quilt flat.

6 Use an eyebrow or lipstick pencil sharpener with two different size openings to maintain sharp points on thick and thin chalk pencils.

7 You can often successfully erase pencil lines from fabric with a white fabric eraser. Avoid using colored erasers or the kinds of erasers found on #2 pencils, which may stain your fabrics with traces of color that won't come out.

8 A hera is a great tool for marking straight quilting designs. This smooth-edged tool marks easy-to-see, straight lines on fabric, which makes it a good choice for marking crosshatched grids.

9 A large, blunt tapestry needle can be used to score straight, easy-to-quilt lines on fabric, and the lines will disappear as you quilt over them.

10 Don't overlook craft shop stencils for quilting designs. Though designed for painted projects, these precut acrylic sheets adapt easily for plain blocks, open areas, and borders, and they dramatically increase your design choices.

11 Freezer paper is one of the best ways to transfer quilting motifs to large quilt borders. Fold and trace the freezer paper to mark identical repeats. Press the freezer paper to the underside of your borders, and trace the designs, using a light box if necessary. Best of all, you can reuse these transfer sheets several times.

12 Here's a markless method: Use freezer paper as a template for quilting simple, isolated shapes. Draw the quilting design onto freezer paper, cut it out, and press it in place on your quilt top using a dry iron. Quilt around the freezer paper shape, then peel it away. For repeated motifs, cut multiple freezer paper templates. Alternately, simple, precut, sticky-back templates are available commercially. Peel off the backing and re-use these paper or fiber shapes several times.

13 Check out the new Sliding Stencils from EZ Quilting. Each stencil consists of two parts that assemble and adjust in length to fit any size quilt border. Corner designs are included where needed for these 4- or 2-inch-wide repeat motifs.

14 Draw accurate cross-hatching lines with a slotted acrylic rotary cutting guide, such as Shape Cut. The narrow channels give you more precision than the wider channels on commercial stencils.

15 If you use wide masking tape to mark quilting lines, be wary of inexpensive discount-store tape, which can leave a residue on your quilt top. A better alternative: low-tack artist's or drafting tape, available in art supply stores. In either case, don't leave tape in place for more than an hour or two.

16 Make a giant light box. Use a rectangular glass-topped table with legs at the corners—this might be a piece of outdoor furniture. Or, open up your dining room table and place a storm window over the opening. Place a lamp on the floor, and let the light shine up through the glass. Tape your quilting design to the glass, position your quilt top over that, and trace your quilting designs onto the fabric.

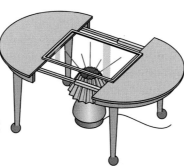

17 Don't forget that a sunny window also makes a great light box. Tape the design to the glass, position the quilt top carefully, and trace the design lines.

18 Put your computer to work as a simple light box: Turn the monitor on and use the plain white screen as a light source. Tape your design and small areas of your quilt top in place, and trace. If you are good with computer graphics, design your quilting motifs on the computer, and play around with scale. Tape the quilt top directly over the screen, and trace.

19 If you will be machine quilting, you might draw your quilting designs onto tissue paper, or use Easy-Tear, a soft and pliable stabilizer, with a permanent marker. Pin or baste the marked design in position on your quilt top. Quilt directly onto the marked design, then gently tear away the stabilizer.

20 Make a reusable transfer for repeat quilting motifs: Stretch tulle or bridal veil in a hoop, and lay it over your design. Trace the design with permanent ink. Now all you need to do is position the marked tulle as desired on your quilt top, and trace the design lines with a soft chalk pencil or washout marker.

It's a Quilt Top—
Now What?

Congratulations! Your quilt top is finished. The colors are magnificent, the points are perfect, and the appliqué is exquisite. Now it's time to choose the quilting designs. This is where many quilters stall. How do you decide what kinds of patterns will work best for your quilt? After spending all the time and effort on your quilt top, you want to be certain that the quilting designs you choose are just right. This chapter offers advice and creative ideas for selecting quilting designs that will enhance your quilts. You'll also learn ways to audition different designs so you'll be confident before taking that first stitch.

Getting Ready

Quilting designs are as important as any other element of a quilt. It is helpful to become familiar with many different styles of quilting before you decide how you want to quilt a quilt. Look through quilting books and magazines for quilting designs, and check out stencils and patterns in quilt shops. Study quilting designs in many different types of quilts: antique, Amish, contemporary, wholecloth, and machine-quilted quilts, plus museum masterpieces, utility quilts, and even miniature quilts. Carry a sketchpad and camera to quilt shows, and make drawings and take close-up photos of quilt designs that intrigue you. Keep a file of inspirational photos of quilting designs. Analyze what you like about these designs, and take notes for future reference. To audition quilting designs, you'll probably want some large pieces of clear plastic; you can purchase Mylar or acetate sheets at your local art supply store.

Completed quilt top

Design wall

Quilting design ideas from your idea file

¼-inch graph paper

Pencil

Eraser

Ruler

Clear Mylar or acetate sheets

Black, fine-tip permanent marker

Colored pencils

Access to a color photocopier

Starting Points

The quilting designs you choose should be compatible with the style of your quilt. **Place the finished quilt top on a design wall** and analyze the style. Is it traditional or contemporary? Pieced, appliquéd, or a combination of both? Is it an antique reproduction? Does it contain folk art elements? Is it a scrap, charm, bargello, watercolor, Baltimore album, or Amish quilt? What kinds of designs have you seen and liked on similar quilts? Keep these patterns and inspirations in mind as you choose your quilting designs.

Purpose of the Quilt

Ask yourself how the quilt is going to be used, how much wear and tear it will receive, and how often it will need to be laundered. **Choose quick-and-easy machine-quilting designs for a baby gift,** a child's "blankey," or a quilt that will be used in a dorm room. Reserve lavish amounts of time and attention for quilting a project that will hang on a wall, or for a beautiful bed quilt that will be admired, appreciated, and well cared for.

A Matter of Time

Tip

Is quilting time at a premium? Check out "Finish It Fast" on page 102.

The amount of time you have to devote to hand or machine quilting should be a factor in determining your quilting designs. If your goal is to have a finished quilt on a bed in a week, select very simple quilting designs that will hold the layers together adequately without requiring many hours to stitch. On the other hand, if you've spent hundreds of hours piecing or appliquéing a very special quilt top, don't skimp on the quilting! Instead, **choose more intricate designs that will function as effective counterpoints to the beauty of your quilt,** and take your time.

Patterns in Prints

Consider the types of fabrics in your quilt top when you think about quilting designs. Large-scale or busy prints will obscure quilting motifs, so **save visually exciting quilting designs, like feathered wreaths or floral motifs, for areas of a quilt featuring solid-color fabrics or quiet tone-on-tone prints. For busier prints, such as these Bow-Tie calicoes, choose simpler quilting options, such as outline quilting,** crosshatch grids, or quilting in the ditch.

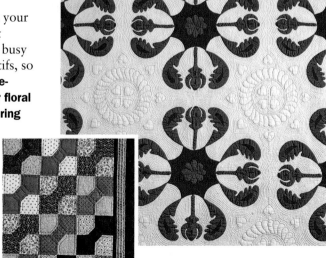

Quilting Skills & Preferences

Your Own Expertise

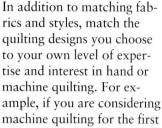

In addition to matching fabrics and styles, match the quilting designs you choose to your own level of expertise and interest in hand or machine quilting. For example, if you are considering machine quilting for the first time, don't choose intricate motifs or patterns. **Instead, stick to simple outline quilting, straight lines, or grids.** If, on the other hand, you're confident in your quilting skills, **challenge yourself with feather designs, or fill backgrounds with meander or stipple quilting.**

For the easiest hand-quilting experience, opt for diagonal lines. Stitching on the bias is easier than on the straight grain.

Machine-Quilting Options

For machine quilting, look for designs that can be stitched continuously, without having to stop frequently to start new lines of stitching. **Follow the lines of a quilting design with one finger. If you can get from beginning to end without ever lifting your finger, it's a continuous-line design.** To stitch continuous-line or other free-motion designs (whether marked or freehand), take some time to practice free-motion quilting and make sure that you feel comfortable with this technique before you begin stitching your project.

Check out your local quilt shop for commercial stencils that are specifically designed for continuous-line machine quilting.

Hand-Quilting Considerations

If you enjoy hand quilting, you'll find a wealth of great design possibilities open to you. **Just about any commercial stencil or pattern in the quilt shop will work for you.** You can use any continuous-line quilting design; however, hand quilting also allows you to work easily with designs that have breaks between the lines. You can easily run a quilting thread from one part of the design to another inside the layer of batting.

Avoid hand quilting a quilt that contains heavyweight fabrics or lots of fusible web. Choose machine quilting for these projects.

IT'S A QUILT TOP—NOW WHAT?

13

Balance & Batting

Tip

Plan quilting around the batting you prefer or choose a batting that's compatible with your quilting designs.

Strive for balance in the quilting throughout your quilt. This does not mean that every inch of the quilt needs to be quilted. **It does mean that if you quilt lines at 2-inch intervals in the center area, you should maintain similar intervals between quilting lines in the border.** If the center of a quilt is quilted more heavily than the border areas, the borders will appear to "do the wave." Remember that different types of batting need to be quilted at different intervals. Always check the packaging for this information.

Repetition & Unity

Tip

For more ideas on creating interesting quilting designs from fabrics, refer to "Let the Fabric Tell You" on page 16.

One effective way to create a feeling of unity throughout a quilt is to repeat one design element in several different areas. **Think about using all or part of an appliqué motif as a quilting design in open areas of your quilt,** or in alternating plain blocks, sashing strips, corner blocks, or an outer border. Also, consider simplifying a design from a favorite theme fabric in the quilt and repeating it as a quilting design.

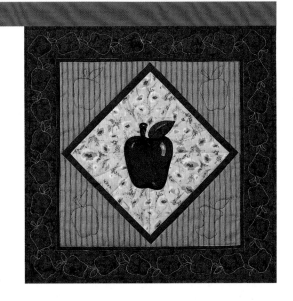

Auditioning Quilting Designs

Line Drawings

Tip

Hang sketches of quilting designs on your refrigerator, where you can see them often, for several days before making your final decisions.

It's a good idea to audition quilting designs before you start quilting, so you're sure you like the choices you've made for your project. To do this, make a scaled-down drawing of your quilt on ¼-inch graph paper, color it in, and make several color photocopies of the page. Using a pencil or a black, fine-tip permanent marker, **sketch in the quilting designs you are considering on your photocopied pages,** and compare them to decide which one you like best.

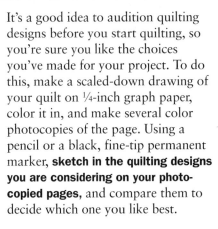

Acetate Overlays

Another good way to audition quilting designs is to use a black, fine-tip permanent marking pen to **trace the quilting designs you are considering onto acetate overlays. Pin your completed quilt top on a design wall and pin the acetates in place.** You'll be able to see at a glance how each design would look on your finished quilt.

Take Polaroids of your quilt top with different quilting designs pinned in various places, and compare them before making your final choices.

Enhancing Patchwork & Appliqué

Dealing with Seams

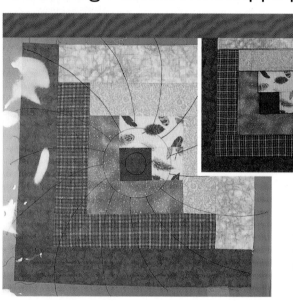

There's no need to view patchwork seams as quilting boundaries. **Quilting in the ditch or ¼ inch away from seams are two options that will allow you to avoid stitching through many layers of fabric and batting,** but these are not the only ways to go when it comes to good design. Try ignoring the seams altogether and **choose quilting designs with flowing curves that go right over pieced seams.** This can soften the angular lines of a pieced design.

Turn to "Patchwork Classics" on page 30 for more creative quilting design options for pieced quilts.

Straight versus Curved Designs

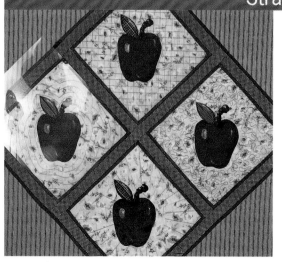

Choose background quilting designs that will enhance the curves of appliqué shapes. Straight lines contrast nicely with curved appliqué motifs. Grid quilting can be single or double and straight or diagonal lines that meet to form squares or diamonds. Lines that radiate out from the center of a block will lead the viewer's eye to an appliqué design, as will the concentric shapes of echo quilting. Random, close stipple quilting creates dense texture in the background and makes the appliqués stand out even more, by contrast.

For more ideas on enhancing appliqué shapes with quilting designs, see "Appliqué Classics" on page 36.

IT'S A QUILT TOP—NOW WHAT?

15

Let the Fabric
Tell You

Finding quilting designs that enhance and carry out the mood or theme of a quilt is not always easy. One solution is to derive quilting motifs from the fabrics you have used in your quilt. Printed and directional fabrics can provide a wealth of great quilting designs. Listen closely: Your fabrics may have some wonderful suggestions for you!

Getting Ready

A multicolor print fabric is a good starting point for coordinating other fabrics for a quilt. This type of fabric can also help you create great quilting designs. Study the print carefully, searching for interesting motifs, and pay close attention to the background areas of the fabric, as well. On graph paper, do some sketches of shapes and designs in the fabric you like. Be curious and ask yourself questions like: What would happen if I deleted a line here or there? Can I alter the curves in a floral motif slightly to make it more appropriate for quilting? What happens if I add an extra line or lines here or there? As you consider questions like these, you'll discover unique quilting designs hidden within the printed motifs of your fabrics.

What You'll Need

Assorted fabrics (include small-, medium-, and large-scale multicolor prints and directionals)

Pencil and paper

Tracing paper

Access to a photocopier with reduce and enlarge functions

Graph paper

Freezer paper

Permanent black marking pen

Clear tape

Long ruler (optional)

Light box (optional)

Opaque projector (optional)

How Fabrics Speak

Solid Partners

Large expanses of solid color in a quilt are perfect places for show-casing fancy quilting designs that will show off your hand- or machine-quilting skills to their best advantage. Look at a multicolor print in your quilt for interesting motifs and designs that you can use in solid-color areas. Maybe you used a gorgeous striped fabric in the borders or an exquisite oriental print in the blocks of your quilt. **Adapt major design elements from the fabric to create beautiful quilting designs for the solid fabrics.**

Motifs in Prints

Tip

Use large-scale prints for alternate plain blocks, and center the motifs carefully in each block so you can quilt around them later.

The simplest way to let fabric "speak" to you about quilting designs is to **choose prints that contain motifs that would make interesting quilting designs.** That way, there's no need to mark the quilt top; all you have to do is **quilt around motifs in the print fabric.**

Continuous Designs

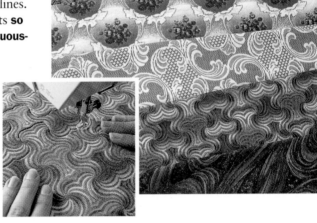

Tip

For easy-to-follow overall patterns, check out fabrics with wavy stripes and other linear designs.

Also, **look for printed fabrics with designs that flow continuously from one element to the next** in unbroken lines. Consider using these in your quilts **so you can free-motion quilt a continuous-line design without marking.**

Back-to-Front Quilting

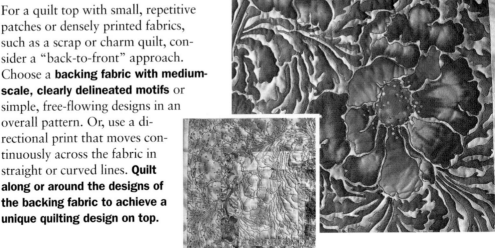

For a quilt top with small, repetitive patches or densely printed fabrics, such as a scrap or charm quilt, consider a "back-to-front" approach. Choose a **backing fabric with medium-scale, clearly delineated motifs** or simple, free-flowing designs in an overall pattern. Or, use a directional print that moves continuously across the fabric in straight or curved lines. **Quilt along or around the designs of the backing fabric to achieve a unique quilting design on top.**

18

Homespun, Shirting & Flannel

With so many great plaids and stripes available in homespun, flannel, and shirting fabrics, it's easy to just follow the straight lines provided by the fabric to produce a quilted grid. Once again, the added benefit is that there's no need to mark the quilt top. Select lines in the fabric that are as close together as you like, or as far apart as recommended for the batting you want to use. **You can also use the lines as guides to quilt lines perpendicular to the stripes, or to quilt diagonal lines that oppose the woven or printed plaid.**

Tip

If you're not confident "eyeballing" perpendicular or diagonal lines, mark these lines on your fabric using a long ruler.

Hand-Dyed Fabrics

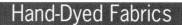

While sometimes subtle, **the gradations or mottlings in hand-dyed fabrics often suggest when to change direction for free-motion quilting designs.** Large-scale abstract prints may suggest playful, meandering quilting designs. Let your imagination have full reign, and think about the potential for quilting stipple designs, clamshells, free-motion waves, or squiggles on these fabrics.

Matching Styles

You can also let fabrics tell you in less literal ways what kinds of quilting designs will look beautiful on a quilt. Instead of outlining motifs or following directional lines, quilt designs that match the feeling generated by your fabric and quilt style. **For a quilt featuring art nouveau fabrics, consider swirly, organic quilting lines.** If your quilt incorporates powerful, contemporary prints in bold colors, consider an overall, oversize, zigzag quilting design to complement the other elements.

LET THE FABRIC TELL YOU

19

Adapting Fabric Designs

Tracing & Simplifying

Tip

A light box makes tracing easy; turn it off to assess the design without the distraction of the photocopy showing through.

Many fabric motifs need to be altered a bit to create effective quilting designs. It's easiest to work from a black-and-white photocopy of the fabric. Begin by tracing only the outline of a motif. **Next, fill in just enough detail so that the design is similar but not identical to the one in the fabric.** Examine your drawn lines to determine whether any are too close together to be distinct from each other after they are quilted. You may need to add lines if some are too far apart. Smooth out lines and round corners if necessary.

Manipulating Scale

Tip

Borrow an opaque projector so you can project images right onto your hanging quilt top and see how they'll look.

When you have captured a quilting design you like on paper, examine it for scale. Is it large enough to fill the planned quilting space? Is it too large? Use a photocopier that can enlarge and reduce images, and play around with the settings **to produce quilting design candidates in several sizes.** Use 11 × 17-inch paper, if necessary. If your design is larger than that, photocopy it in sections and tape the pages together to create the finished design.

Successful Repetition

Tip

See "Simple Shapes, Super Effects!" on page 52 for inspiration on using the motifs you traced from your fabrics.

Repeating an image is another way to make a motif fit a space. Cut a piece of freezer paper to the same size and shape as the area you want to fill. Fold the paper in half, or into quarters or eighths. **Trace your quilting design onto each section of the freezer paper,** positioning it to form pleasing repeats. **Or run motifs continuously around a block or border. To create mirror-image motifs, refold the paper and trace the motifs again.**

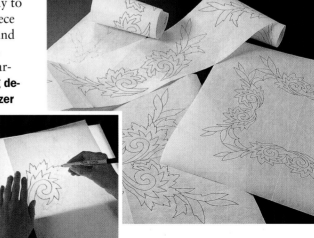

The Quilter's
Problem Solver

Go for Balance

Problem	Solution
The quilting design you've drawn from your fabric will result in quilting that is too dense in some areas.	Analyze the design. Are there interior lines that can be eliminated? If not, try deleting entire elements within the pattern, and find a simpler motif that would fit better in that space.
You need to add more quilting so that the density of the quilting will be balanced.	Return to your fabric, and look for other motifs that can be added to expand your quilting design options. Sometimes you'll find suitable smaller motifs in the background area of a print. Also, consider filling in background areas with crosshatched grids.
Your theme fabric is a wild frog print, but you don't want to quilt frogs on your quilt.	Fabrics from the same collection or in the same theme may suggest related motifs. Look for things associated with frogs, such as lily pads, water ripples, dragonflies, or other designs. Modify these to create suitable quilting designs.
You've created a great floral design for your blocks, but it doesn't lend itself to the sashing and corner squares.	Isolated motifs from your design can be quite pleasing when rearranged in different configurations. Just try to keep them in scale with each other. For instance, use a smaller floral design in the corner squares. Then mark and quilt a row of leaves in the sashing strips. Make sure the leaves are proportioned to match the flower used in the corner square.

Skill Builder

Check the library for reference books on fabrics.

Look for examples of great textiles from various time periods, and see which ones have designs that look close to the style of your quilt. This kind of search can be very enjoyable and can often yield surprising and wonderful ideas for quilting designs.

Try This!

Why not think *big*?

Look for giant-scale prints when planning your quilt. You can quilt inside and around the motifs, which will give the impression that the design is lavishly appliquéd, rather than printed. You can also reduce the motifs on a photocopier to produce miniature versions. When used in plain blocks and borders, these echoes of the large motifs will unify your quilt nicely.

LET THE FABRIC TELL YOU

Planning Around
Quilting Designs

Any patchwork or appliqué quilt can take on the artistry and elegance of Sunday best when the quilting designs are tailored to the quilt. Rather than waiting until after your quilt top is completed to think about how you want to quilt it, take the opposite approach. Coordinate the quilting designs with the patchwork or appliqué patterns of your quilt right from the start. The secret to perfect harmony lies in thinking about both of these elements at the same time, as soon as you start planning a quilt.

Getting Ready

Give careful thought to the quilt pattern you want to work with and to quilting designs that will be compatible with it. It is very helpful to spend time looking through magazines, patterns, photos of quilts, and books of full-size quilting designs to help you decide what kinds of quilts and quilting designs you like. (Diane Gaudynski's award-winning October Morning, shown opposite, is a prime example of a quilt planned with the quilting patterns in mind.) Sit at a large worktable where you can spread out several books or magazines at a time and where you can work comfortably with quilting stencils, freezer paper, pencils, felt-tip pens, art erasers, and a compass or circle templates.

Diane Gaudynski's October Morning, on the opposite page, and in details below and on page 24, is a part of the collection of the Museum of the American Quilter's Society (MAQS), Paducah, KY; photo by Richard Walker, © MAQS.

Patterns for pieced or appliqué quilts

Books showing quilting designs on similar quilts

Books of full-size quilting designs

Quilting stencils or appliqué designs

Compass or circle templates

Assortment of acrylic rulers

Pencil

Art eraser

Freezer paper

Drawing paper

Permanent black fine-tip pen

Straight pins

Quilting Considerations

Fabric Factors

When you think about making a quilt, keep in mind that the fabrics you choose for the quilt will play an important part in determining the quilting designs. **Choose fabrics that will allow you to use the quilting designs you like or quilting designs that will complement the fabrics you select.** For example, if you wish to quilt a crosshatch grid, consider quiet prints. Avoid woven or printed plaid patterns if you think the quilting lines will conflict with the lines in the fabric.

White Space

From the start, plan on including some "white space" in your quilt—plain areas with no piecing or appliqué—that you can devote solely to quilting designs. White space gives the viewer's eye a place to rest in pieced or appliquéd designs; it sometimes occurs naturally in certain blocks or designs, **as in this Delectable Mountains medallion, where half of the space is plain.** In these areas, be sure to use a fabric that is solid or that reads as a solid.

Specific Stencils

You can customize the size of certain spaces in a quilt to incorporate specific quilting designs you want to use. For example, if you want to include a cable design of a specific width in your sashing strips, **cut the sashing strips to accommodate the stencil.** This is easier than altering the stencil. You can build these measurements into a quilt at the planning stage and make the marking process simple later. This preplanning takes away laborious mathematical calculations or guesswork.

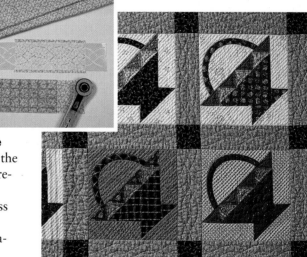

Echoes

For overall balance, it's a good idea to repeat quilting designs throughout a quilt. These designs can recur in different sizes. For example, you can use a smaller clamshell as a background and a larger one in the border. You can also echo the same type of curved line in different designs. **Here, the scalloped lines of a clamshell design that create texture in the flower basket of this quilt resemble the shape and curves of the feathers in the border.**

Tip

Repeat or echo an element from a patchwork or appliqué design in the quilting to reinforce a design theme.

Proportion

You can plan the size of your entire quilt to fit the quilting designs you wish to use. **This 15-inch-square miniature wholecloth quilt showcases a variety of small quilting patterns.** The larger-scale, four-petaled flower in the center and the feathers with hearts are similar in scale. The medium-scale diagonal lines and the small, dense stippling around the edges make for a nice contrast. Vary the scale of your quilting designs throughout a quilt; a little variety goes a long way toward adding interest, no matter how small or large your quilt is.

Tip

Purchase a commercial wholecloth quilt pattern. Make alterations to personalize it and see how many unique variations you can create.

Density

Distribute densely quilted areas evenly over your quilt, and your quilt will lie flat, straight, and true. **If you decide on densely quilted background areas in the borders, be sure to include quilting designs of similar density throughout the rest of the quilt.** If the center of a quilt is more closely quilted than the border areas, the borders will not lie flat. And if the quilting lines are spaced at wide intervals in the center and the borders are heavily quilted, the edges will pull in and cause the center portion to balloon out.

Traffic Signals

Attention—feathers ahead! Just like traffic signs, quilting designs can act as signs that guide the viewer's eye to something you want to accentuate. **For example, quilted feathers around an appliqué shape can make it seem more visually prominent.** Think about encircling an area of your quilt with a quilting design so the eye moves all around the area you wish to highlight. In patchwork patterns, lines of quilting may emphasize the overall shapes or designs, or they may create a sense of movement.

Final Preparations

Designing for Fit

Tip

For a symmetrical quilting design, create a freezer paper pattern that corresponds to one quadrant of the entire quilt top.

When you have decided on the quilting designs that you will use, cut and piece your quilt top to be sure of the space allotments before finalizing your quilting designs. Take finished measurements in order to prepare full-size freezer paper patterns for each area of the quilt top. Draw one large repeat section, such as half of one side. Include corner squares and any adjacent spaces, such as setting triangles. **Draw dashed lines through the center of triangles and squares to help you position and align the repeats accurately.**

Sketching & Finalizing

Tip

Remember: After ironing freezer paper patterns to the back of your quilt top, the designs you trace will be reversed.

Sketch your full-size quilting designs on paper, and play with placements in each design area on the freezer paper. Combine, tilt, or rotate motifs, leaving ½ inch between the designs and the seams or appliqués in your quilt. Pin your sketches to a wall and see how they look. Enlarge or reduce quilting designs, and keep adding, subtracting, and rearranging quilting lines until you achieve the look you like. When you are happy with the quilting designs, **trace over them with a black fine-tip pen so you can trace them onto your quilt top.**

Making Quilted Samples

Tip

For the best preview, pin the samples right over the corresponding areas on your quilt top.

It can often be helpful to actually quilt some full-size samples of your chosen designs before taking the final step and marking them on your quilt top. **Quilt several samples, such as a block design, background area,** border section, setting square, or sashing strip. Pin them on a design wall and stand back to see how you like them. This process will tell you whether the scales are appropriate, whether you will enjoy quilting them, and whether they will be too time-consuming or too difficult for your skill level.

The Quilter's
Problem Solver

Keeping Quilting Designs Prominent

Problem	Solution
The isolated motifs you quilted get lost in your background quilting.	There should be good contrast of scale between background quilting lines and the lines of an individual or isolated quilting motif. For example, with a floral design, use meander quilting much smaller in scale than the individual flowers and leaves. Or contrast straight quilting lines with a curved quilt design (and vice versa). Straight lines such as crosshatching will generally enhance floral or other curved motifs.
The motif you're using in the border looks lost in the larger corner areas.	Embellish the same design, expanding it with similar or complementary elements. For example, a classic urn in the center of a border might, in its corner placement, have more flowers spilling out of it. You can almost always frame or enhance a design with feathers.

Skill Builder

Pin-prick full-size quilting designs from a finished quilt.

If you've found a quilting design you adore on another quilt, you can easily copy it by placing the quilt over a piece of freezer paper, shiny side down, on top of a soft surface (such as a piece of flannel). Using a silk pin that won't damage the quilt, push the pin through the quilt and the freezer paper underneath, perforating the paper. Do this every ¼ inch around the entire quilting design, and remove the quilt from the paper. Connect the tiny holes in the paper with a permanent black fine-tip pen. The design is then ready to trace onto your own quilt.

Try This!

Add complexity to background grid lines.

Instead of simply quilting crosshatch grids in the background of an appliqué block, borrow a motif from the appliqué design itself, and insert it into your pattern of background quilting lines. Use a small appliqué motif such as a rose, several leaves, or any isolated floral motif. Arrange motifs symmetrically or sprinkle them randomly throughout a background area. Such details serve to break up crosshatched grid lines and give your quilt greater visual interest without overpowering the appliqué design.

**Quilting Designs
from October Morning,**
by Diane Gaudynski

**Hare Pattern
by Jeana Kimball**

Patchwork
Classics

A quilting design for patchwork should enhance your quilt without taking star status away from the pieced pattern. No matter whether your quilt is traditional or innovative, or whether you like to stitch by hand or machine, it's always worthwhile to consider lots of ideas before you focus in on your favorite. Scope out the creative quilting choices in this chapter and see how many more you can think up on your own. You may wind up with more quilting designs than quilts to be quilted!

Getting Ready

The first step in choosing quilting designs for a patchwork quilt is to take a good look at your completed quilt top. Hang it up if it's going to go on a wall, or put it on a table or bed if the end result will be viewed horizontally. Carefully analyze the elements of the pieced design. Read "It's a Quilt Top—Now What?" on page 10, think about the general considerations, and use either of the auditioning techniques described in that chapter to try out possible designs.

The quilt top used throughout this chapter features the Variable Star block (also called Ohio Star or Evening Star). The stars are assembled in rows rather than as separate blocks, and without sashing strips in order to allow more unseamed, open spaces for quilting designs. Consider how the ideas suggested here might work with any patchwork quilt top and how you might adapt these and other designs to suit *your* quilt top.

Read "It's a Quilt Top—Now What?" on page 10

What You'll Need

Patchwork quilt top

Paper

Pencils

Colored pencils

¼-inch graph paper

Large, clear acetate sheets

Fine-tip permanent marker

Tried & True Approaches

Outline Options

To emphasize the pieced pattern of a block itself, **quilting ¼ inch from the seam lines of the pattern is always effective. In addition, you can quilt the pieced design (perhaps on a different scale) in the empty spaces.** These approaches will strengthen the graphic quality of a patchwork pattern and show off your piecing as well as your quilting skills.

Expand on the pieced design by adding more lines, or simplify a more complex block by deleting lines.

PATCHWORK CLASSICS

Plain Areas First

Tip

Use masking tape as a guide to quilting diagonal lines behind the curved motif.

A simple curved motif, such as a four-petaled flower, can be used to create interesting quilting designs that will enhance a pieced quilt top. **Start by marking motifs in the centers of your alternate plain blocks or in any other open areas. Add diagonal lines, squares, and rectangles to fill in the areas around the pieced designs.** You can often create interesting effects by disregarding the seam lines of your pieced blocks.

Tradition on the Wing

Tip

Diagonally halve a square patch from your quilt to determine a good size for a triangle shape to quilt.

Consider using a traditional patchwork shape, like the popular Flying Geese triangle, as a quilting design. Decide which way you would like your quilted "geese" to fly, and quilt the motifs repetitively in that direction. **Flying Geese triangles can be even more effective if you overlap them or place them so they "fly" right over the border** in straight or curved lines.

Channel Quilting

Tip

Channel quilt in different directions in different areas of your quilt.

Channel quilting is a simple way to enhance the lines of a patchwork quilt. It consists of single, double, or triple parallel lines, which can be either straight or curved. **You can space lines of channel quilting any distance apart that you like (refer to the quilting requirements of your batting), placing them horizontally, vertically, or diagonally.** Channels are easy to stitch and produce a strong, dramatic look in blocks, sashing strips, and borders. When you use double channels in both directions, you can create an interesting background grid design.

Alternating Designs

Alternate geometric patterns from block to block. On the first row, mark a pattern of four crosshatch lines, forming nine-patch divisions in every other square. Fill in the remaining squares with five equally spaced diagonal lines, all slanting in the same direction. On the next row, mark the first block with diagonal lines, alternating blocks with crosshatched lines. **By alternating these two designs from row to row, with the lines intersecting along the square units, your quilting design will form diagonal chains.**

Add a stand-alone chain or cable design to wind around the border. This will echo the design in the interior of your quilt and unify the overall design.

Fun & Games—Xs & Os

Inject some fun into your quilt—choose a pattern of Xs and Os. The significance of Xs and Os, or "hugs and kisses," guarantees that your finished quilt will make a wonderful gift for a loved one. **Quilt the blocks in a pattern of concentric circles and diagonally crossed lines.** If you have a nine-patch arrangement, you might think of the blocks in your quilt top as a big tic-tac-toe board. Where you place the Xs and Os is up to you!

For extra emphasis, quilt the words "hugs and kisses" or "tic-tac-toe" repeatedly around the border.

Block-over-Block Designs

Superimpose a traditional block design as the quilting design over a different pieced block. **Choose a simple block, like Pinwheel or Square within a Square.** Use simple blocks within each square grid of your pieced block, or superimpose a more complex one over the entire block. Audition possibilities on graph paper or clear plastic sheets. Another way to try out designs is to photocopy a drawing of the actual-size block several times and sketch different quilting designs on each one.

Check an encyclopedia of block patterns for block designs that might be compatible with your patchwork.

Block-over-Quilt Designs

For a repeat-block pieced quilt, consider enlarging the block pattern itself until it is large enough to fit over the entire quilt top, or at least within the borders. **The Variable Star is effective as a single gigantic quilting motif, perhaps defined by cross-hatched lines inside the lines of the design.** Fill in the background areas around the large quilted Variable Star with a smaller, curved quilting pattern, such as clamshells or another texture that contrasts nicely with the giant star.

Innovative Approaches

Radiating Lines

Tip

For a small quilt, avoid marking more than three starting points, or the result could be too many lines that look jumbled.

For an unusual spin on straight-line quilting, select a point on your quilt top that you'd like to focus on. (Sometimes off-center is more interesting than dead center.) **Then mark radiating lines out in all directions from this point.** These radiating lines can stop at the border or go right to the edges. You can add radiating lines that stop short of the dense center, or use more than one starting point; an odd number usually looks best.

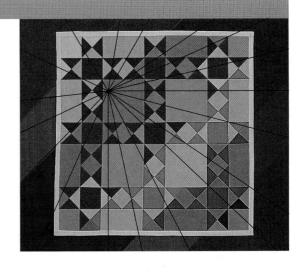

Quilt Me a Picture

Think of your quilt top as a blank slate for a picture entirely independent from the piecing. Or let the shapes and lines of the piecing design simply suggest certain pictorial forms. **For example, triangles and rectangles in a pieced star design might inspire a cottage in the woods,** or a boat on the water. Fill in the shapes with lively details; quilt windows, doors, and shingles on a house, and add smoke curling out of the chimney. Design the picture so the density of quilting will be balanced throughout the quilt.

PATCHWORK CLASSICS

Freehand Motifs

Freehand quilting designs make a wonderful counterbalance to the rigidity of a pieced design. Decide on a shape you would enjoy quilting, such as stars, suns, leaves, or circles, and **mark them freehand, in several different sizes, all over your quilt top.** Start with the largest motifs, and fill in the spaces between them with medium-size and smaller motifs.

Tip

Use a freehand version of your patchwork pattern to free-motion quilt your design in no time flat!

Creating Panels

Divide your quilt top into three or four vertical or horizontal sections and quilt each section or alternate sections in different patterns. **Undulating vines are fun to quilt, and they make an interesting foil for angular, pieced patches.** You can make your designs as simple or as complex as you like, depending on how much quilting you want to do. Draw the designs freehand, using a French curve to mark smoothly flowing lines. Or use commercial stencils or quilting patterns that appeal to you.

Medallion Effect

A medallion-type quilt design, either patchwork or appliqué, features a strong center motif surrounded by successive, concentric additional designs in different scales. Try using this concept as the basis for your quilting design. **This basket of flowers is framed by channels, diagonal lines, isolated basket motifs, and floral vines and crosshatched grids in the border.** You can create a medallion and surrounding designs with any motifs in any size you like; just be sure to include a variety of designs for greatest visual appeal.

PATCHWORK CLASSICS

35

A ppliqué quilts offer wonderful opportunities for showcasing stunning quilting designs. Fill background spaces with elaborate designs, such as feathered wreaths or baskets overflowing with flowers, using the appliqués themselves as inspiration. On the other hand, simple background patterns or textures can be just as effective when you want to emphasize fine appliqué work. You can achieve numerous beautiful looks for your appliqué quilt by adopting any of the ideas offered in this chapter. Pull up a comfortable chair and consider a wide range of possibilities.

Getting Ready

Look through books that feature beautiful appliqué quilts, both new and antique. Make photocopies of designs you like and keep them in a file, along with photos of appliqué quilts that appeal to you. After you finish making an appliqué quilt top, check your file for quilts with a similar style, and notice the quilting designs they contain. Always plan on auditioning lots of ideas before making your final choices. While the quilt top in this chapter features a straight setting without sashing strips, you can still consider many of the quilting options here for use in on-point sets and other styles of quilts. Refer to page 14 in "It's a Quilt Top—Now What?" for ways to audition these quilting designs for your quilt top.

Traditional Favorites

Outline & Ditch Quilting

The simplest, most basic way to quilt any appliqué quilt is to outline quilt around individual motifs and stitch-in-the-ditch between blocks, sashing strips, and borders. This minimal quilting makes the appliqué shapes stand out and anchors the three layers of the quilt together. And because you're merely following edges and seams, there is no need for marking.

Diagonal Lines

Many of our quilting foremothers liked to quilt the background of an appliqué quilt in a pattern of diagonal lines. This traditional approach holds the layers of the quilt securely together and promotes durability. **The diagonal lines around the outline quilted appliqués enhances and brings out the shapes of the appliqué motifs.**

The Inside Track

Another way to enhance your appliqués is to quilt on top of them. **Stitching ¼ inch *inside* the edges of each of the individual appliqué shapes in the quilt is a uniform way to emphasize their shapes.** Because the quilting lines echo the curves and add texture, they heighten the visual interest of the appliqué. Straight-line background quilting (such as the diagonal crosshatching inside the wreath) and channel quilting outside make good foils for the quilted curves atop the appliqués.

Border Repeats

Diagonal and crosshatched lines in the background will cause these background areas to recede, bringing the appliqué shapes forward visually. To further enhance the appliqué design, **use your appliqué templates to mark quilting designs in the border, spacing them as you like. Quilt the outline of these same motifs in the borders.**

Stippling

Whether you like to stitch by hand or machine, try stipple quilting in the background areas of an appliquéd quilt. The closeness of stipple quilting flattens the surface, and by contrast, an appliqué motif will stand out attractively. Contrast the curvy meanderings of stippling with a crisp cross-hatch pattern in a different background area.

Ripple Effects

Echo quilting adds a sense of movement that complements curved appliqué shapes. **Filling background areas with curved lines of quilting that repeat the outlines of the appliqué motifs will continually draw the viewer's eye back to the appliqué shapes.** Lines may be consistently ¼ inch or ½ inch apart, but you can also create interesting effects by varying these intervals. Echo quilting resembles water rippling gently. To emphasize this theme, quilt a related pattern in the borders of the quilt, such the conch shells shown here.

Tip

If you are comfortable eyeballing lines within and around shapes, there's no need to mark for echo quilting.

Subtle Repetitions

For a feeling of unity, echo the general shape of the appliqué motifs in quilting designs. The quilting design inside the wreath hints at the shapes of the appliquéd flowers. And where four blocks meet to create a larger expanse of background, the entire appliqué design can be repeated in a quilted design. Simplify the design and change the scale to fit the space.

Tip

Consider alternating the directions of channel quilting from one block to another.

APPLIQUÉ CLASSICS

Garden Influences

Tip

Look closely at the detail on page 106 to see how stippling enhances a quilted holly-leaf motif.

The four-branched sprig of leaves in the areas between blocks and the leafy border vine give a floral appliqué quilt the look of a formal garden with balance, symmetry, and grace. If you want to go one step further, use stipple quilting, either by hand or with free-motion stitching by machine, to add dense texture around each quilted motif. As the stipple quilting flattens an area, the less densely quilted motifs will puff out by contrast and seem trapuntoed.

Innovative Twists

Changing Directions

Tip

Guide the viewer's eye back to the appliquéd motifs by adding a small, curved quilting design inside the wreaths.

Consider quilting directional lines within each block to create secondary background patterns where the blocks meet. **To do this, quilt parallel, evenly spaced diagonal lines that originate at each of the corners of the blocks.** This will result in a pattern with a trellislike effect that is especially lovely for setting off garden and floral motifs. These diagonal shifts will keep your eye moving across the surface of the quilt. Continue the same diagonal lines into the borders, forming a chevron-type design.

Magnificent Medallions

Even if your appliquéd quilt is a repeat block or Baltimore album–style design, the quilting designs you choose can give it a unique and interesting medallion look. To emphasize the center, mark and **quilt an elaborate corner quilting design on all sides of the center block.** Feature an equally attention-getting design around the border. Elsewhere, use quiet repeats like feathered wreaths in the centers of appliqué wreaths and a subtle background design such as a diagonal grid.

Patchwork Style

The angular lines of a pieced pattern can make great quilting designs for appliqué quilts. Choose a patchwork design you like and reduce or enlarge it to fit the plain areas around appliqué designs. Quilt a portion of the design or a reduced version inside the appliqué area. **Continue the quilting in the border or other areas as needed, using straight lines to complement the patchwork motifs.**

Wavy Channels

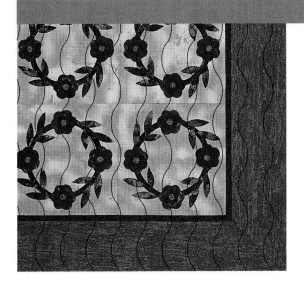

Try an interesting twist on channel quilting. **Mark curved lines of channel quilting using a stencil or self-made template. Keep the undulations regular, parallel, and equally spaced.** This wavy channel quilting will subtly echo the curves of the appliqué shapes.

Oversize Designs

Consider using an oversize circular wreath design as a huge quilting motif that will cover the quilt center inside the border. Add crosshatching lines inside and diagonal channel quilting in other background areas, as counterpoints to the curved lines. Run a similar curved design around the border, to frame the center appropriately.

APPLIQUÉ CLASSICS

Great *Inspirations*

Who says that quilting designs have to come from quilt books, patterns, or
magazines? Good designs are all around you! Look closely at everyday items for
interesting patterns that adorn china, wood, metal, leather, and plastic. Many
wonderful graphics that come from outside the realm of quiltmaking can inspire you to adapt
quilting designs or create entirely new ones. Think outside the box, and you'll enhance your
quilts with the most unique, interesting, and appropriate designs you could ever imagine.

Getting Ready

Capture beautiful ideas as you come across them by taking a camera or sketchbook with you everywhere you go. Check out interesting architectural details of public and private buildings. Notice patterns in tile, linoleum, carpeting, rugs, floorcloths, parquet, and hardwood grain. Look at beautiful works of art. Leaf through wallpaper catalogs. Pay attention to commercial packaging. You'll be surprised by all the inspiration you find.

Keep a file of magazine clippings, photos, sketches, and so on, that could be modified and made into quilting designs. This file can be as simple as a manila envelope, or as complex as a series of folders labeled with different styles or motifs. Whenever you finish a quilt top, go to your idea file and experiment with various designs, adapting them to suit the way you want your quilt to look.

Unexpected Sources

Greeting Cards

Spend some time looking at greeting cards. Do the designs give you ideas for quilting designs? Choose simple motifs and clean lines. Consider whether some lines could be eliminated while leaving the graphic identifiable. The coffee cups on this card have distinct lines that could easily be quilted, and the square shape lends itself to use on an alternate block. Be especially aware of copyright, however, and use copyrighted images for inspiration only. It is illegal to reproduce illustrations and artwork line for line without express permission.

Tip

Valentines are rich in inspiration for wedding and anniversary quilts.

GREAT INSPIRATIONS

Copyright-Free Books

Tip

Hunt in used bookstores for books containing Victorian designs, gothic illustrations, and storybook pictures.

Some design books are copyright-free and are intended for needleworkers and artists to use in their work. Look for books like these at needlework shops, art stores, and bookstores. They are usually quite inexpensive, and they provide a wide range of lovely designs that can be easily adapted to quilting patterns. **Select motifs from a design, and group them in different configurations, eliminating or adding background lines where necessary to fit the spaces in your quilt.**

Household Items

Tip

If you prefer not to sketch motifs free-hand, photocopy the item, enlarging as desired, and trace designs from the copy.

Both fine china and everyday dinnerware often feature marvelous designs that would enhance patchwork or appliqué. **The simple floral pattern around a plate could be used to form a wreath around an appliqué motif,** vines around a border, or embellishments for sashing strips. Take a closer look at other household items in your kitchen and dining room, too—painted or etched glass, tin, and wood; the handles of silverware; or butter and cookie presses.

Trinkets & Treasures

Tip

Filigree designs in jewelry can be enlarged to produce lovely, intricate, continuous quilting designs.

Many decorative objects are cherished because their designs appeal to both the heart and the eye. Liberate yourself from the notion that you must use designs intact. Pick out individual elements that appeal to you, such as the leaves and flower from the lid of a miniature cache box. **Use these as isolated motifs or in a different arrangement that suits the space you want to fill in a quilt.** Your finished quilting designs may turn out quite different from the original images that inspired them.

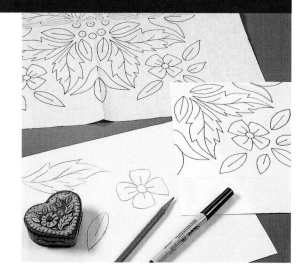

GREAT INSPIRATIONS

Architectural Details

Take a walk around your town and notice the gingerbread moldings, shingle patterns, keystones, marble trim, and other architectural details on buildings. **Take a camera with you and shoot photos of things that would make appealing quilting designs.** If you have a telephoto lens or setting, use it to get close-up shots. Enlarge good candidates for quilting designs on a photocopier, and **trace the designs onto tracing paper.**

Look down, too! Decorative tiles, brickwork, parquet and inlaid marble floors, linoleum, carpeting, and rugs can all inspire great quilting designs.

Seals & Stamps

The United States Presidential Seal on a passport was modified for this quilt, "Let Freedom Ring." **The bald eagle was enlarged on a photocopier and adapted** so that the design would fit a large triangular space. In addition to embossed seals, consider the wide range of rubber stamps now available in any theme you can imagine. Many stamped designs would be very effective as quilting designs.

Holiday Decorations

Christmas ornaments and accessories are rich sources of perfect motifs for quilts to deck your halls with style. **Tape tracing paper around a curved surface so you can trace designs and produce a flat version,** or make a "rubbing" with a soft lead pencil if the design is raised. Czech Easter eggs, incised gourds, and decorated column candles may offer ideas for quilts that celebrate other seasons and special occasions.

Party stores carry die-cut tinsel shapes in many themes for wire garlands. Enlarge these shapes to create a great border design.

GREAT INSPIRATIONS

Getting the
Heirloom Look

I f you love traditional-style quilts and antiques, avoid contemporary quilting designs on a quilt top with old-fashioned patterns and nostalgic fabrics. Instead of selecting designs from commercial stencils or other modern-day sources, let quilt historian Joe Cunningham explain how to incorporate nineteenth-century quilting designs into your projects. You'll end up with a wonderful vintage look and a quilt that looks as if it has been in your family for generations.

Getting Ready

Creating a new quilt with an heirloom look involves thinking like a quilter from an earlier era. In the nineteenth century, quilts needed to be quilted closely to hold homemade batting together, and quilters had to create their quilting designs without the help of fancy marking tools, commercial templates, or stencils. To get yourself into an "antique" frame of mind, gather some books or calendars with pictures of antique quilts from before 1900. Use a magnifying glass to examine the quilting designs. Make sketches of designs that appeal to you, and take notes about various quilting patterns and techniques that might work well in your own quilts.

The quilts in this chapter, antiques borrowed mostly from the collection of Judy Roche, will give you a sampling of quilting designs from nineteenth century quilts, especially from the Delaware and Lancaster Counties of Pennsylvania.

What You'll Need

Books and magazines showing antique quilts

Pencils

Paper

Magnifying glass

Homages to History

Batting Options

The modern-day quilter who decided to quilt this 1830s quilt top probably stopped midstitch, realizing that her batting was too puffy. Part of getting an heirloom look is using low-loft cotton batting; in old quilts, it tended to break apart and make small "pillows" that were enclosed by close quilting. Today there are a number of thin, 100 percent cotton batts available that are very easy to quilt. **To simulate a vintage look, opt for one of these batts, rather than a higher-loft polyester, which creates a more contemporary look in a quilt.**

Match Styles

Tip

Stitching-in-the-ditch is another more modern approach to avoid when pursuing a vintage look.

For an heirloom look, match your quilting style to the quilt style. For example, if you have made a quilt similar to **this pre-1940s Amish quilt, choose Amish quilting designs.** Feathered vines, crosshatching, cables, and simple florals are typical of traditional Amish quilts. For traditional pieced quilts, avoid outline quilting. Nineteenth-century quilts almost always have lines through patches instead of ¼-inch outlines in them. Criss-cross through each patch or just put a series of lines through the section.

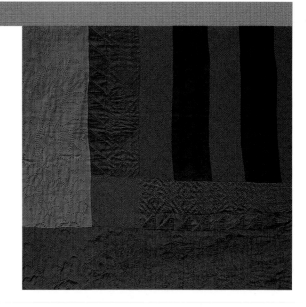

Close Quilting

From 1800 to 1900, there was a fairly steady progression from **very small-scale quilting designs with lines about ⅓ or ½ inch apart, like this quilt (circa 1860),** to larger-scale quilting designs with lines about 1 to 2 inches apart. Modern quilts and battings do not need such close quilting, but if you want to give your quilt an antique look, choose designs that feature close lines of quilting.

Allover Fans

Baptist Fan was a popular pattern in the nineteenth century. **As in this Apple Tree quilt, made between 1875 and 1900, fan designs were often started in one bottom corner and stitched diagonally to the other corner.** Quilters sometimes worked from all corners toward the center, filling in with smaller fans wherever necessary. Quilters used string or even their arms to scribe these arcs! Arching curves such as these also add a distinctively heirloom look to patchwork, and the quilted curves will add softness to an angular piecing design.

Double & Triple Lines

Nineteenth-century quilters often gave added emphasis to quilting designs by doubling or tripling design lines, as in this Eight Pointed Star quilt made in Maryland in the 1840s. Similarly, diagonal lines in groups of two or three, or double grid lines, either square or on the diagonal, create a more old-fashioned look than single lines would. Doubling up the lines for feathers, flowers, vines, or other classic quilting designs also gives an heirloom look to your quilting. Quilt the grouped lines less than ¼ inch from each other.

Tip

Mark just one set of lines on a quilt and use those as a guide for eye-balling the distance to additional, close quilting lines.

Freehand Quilting

In the nineteenth century, quilting designs were usually not as carefully planned or marked as today. To create the look of an earlier era, quilt as much as possible freehand. Almost any design can be quilted without marking, if you're willing to give it a try. Start with straight-line designs, like the ones in this Amish hired man's Nine-Patch quilt from 1825. Irregularities give this quilt a person-ality all its own. Accept the inevitable slight wanderings of your needle, which will add charm to your quilt.

Tip

Visualize a line diagonally connecting opposite corners of your patches, and quilt this line freehand.

Right over the Design

Nowadays we tend to think of quilting as something that reinforces the pattern of a quilt. However, our quilting foremothers often quilted de-signs that covered the entire surface of a quilt, without regard to pieced or appliquéd patterns. In the early part of the nineteenth century, especially in certain regions, quilters would often ignore the appliqué pattern and quilt right over it in an allover pattern, as shown in this circa 1890 quilt. This treatment is rarely seen these days, and would certainly bestow a vintage look upon a new quilt.

Tip

Cut away the excess fabric behind your appliqués so you'll have fewer layers to quilt through.

GETTING THE HEIRLOOM LOOK

49

Outlining Appliqués

As appreciation for quilting skills grew to rival that for fine hand appliqué, quilts featured outline quilting close around the appliqué shapes and often within each shape, as well. **This Pomegranate quilt from the 1870s is a good example.** To simulate this look, quilt less than ¼ inch outside and inside of the appliqué shapes. For larger appliqués, quilt smaller, concentric echoes, such as those found on the large leaves. Close lines of crosshatching in the background provide a nice foil to the outline quilting.

Isolated Motifs

Nineteenth-century quilters often quilted flowers, leaves, or feather designs wherever they felt like it and did not try to echo or reinforce piecing or appliqué designs. **Notice the man and woman (possibly a bride and groom), the heart, and the posy design in the corner of this Ohio Whig Rose quilt, circa 1870–80.** When you finish a quilt top, consider quilting it without a clear, overall plan that relates to the quilt style; simply fill in spaces however you like, quilting isolated motifs, straight lines, and freehand lines as you go.

Classic Designs

To give your quilt immediate yesteryear charm, look to crosshatching, cables, and feathers. Grids or crosshatching brought crispness. For more graceful lines, feathers were favorites as they are today. And thirdly, **cables were extremely popular, as shown in this Oak Leaf and Reel quilt from 1875.** Instead of working out a fancy corner resolution so that all four corners of a quilt were identical and the quilting design continuous, corner designs were often interrupted, or chopped off, as shown here.

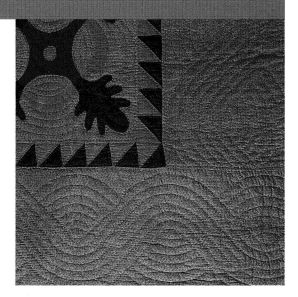

The Quilter's
Problem Solver

Pleasing Discrepancies

Problem	Solution
You marked allover fan designs on your quilt top, but the patterns did not come out even at the edges of the quilt.	Fans are groups of concentric arcs. The first part of the solution is realizing that you will always end up with a partial unit somewhere on your quilt. If you want to minimize these partial units, make all of your fans go in one direction, and make sure that the fan unit is a size that divides evenly into your quilt's dimensions. That way you will have partial units only on one side.
I'm tempted to use contrasting thread to quilt plain white blocks. Will this give me "antique" appeal?	Contrasting thread will certainly make quilting stitches show up more than white thread would. If you are striving for an antique look, however, the softer appearance of white-on-white will be more typical of old-fashioned quilts.
How do you age a new quilt to give it a vintage feel?	Nothing "antiques" a new quilt like washing it. If your quilt is solidly made, with ¼-inch seam allowances and new, prewashed fabric, it can be put in the washing machine on a gentle cycle, with no soap. To soften the batting and create a crinkled antique look, put it through a gentle cycle in the dryer. Of course, no antique quilt should ever be washed in a machine.

Skill Builder

If you're self-conscious about your large quilting stitches, focus on the evenness of your stitches and the distance between them.

Using large stitches, stitch some fans freehand. Many old quilts from the rural South are quilted this way. A contrasting color thread, while not the typical choice of days gone by, will allow you to gauge each stitch visually. It won't be long before your stitches march evenly along any type of quilting pattern you select.

Try This!

Do some nineteenth-century machine crosshatching.

Early machine quilters almost always used a simple grid over the entire quilt, often quilting right across appliqué or pieced designs. Make the task easy and the results precise: Measure and mark—or apply masking tape—for the first line in each direction, then attach a sewing guide to your machine to stitch the others. Diagonal lines are the easiest to stitch: quilt one set of diagonals across a quilt, then stitch a second set of lines perpendicular to it. An on-point grid of squares ¾ inch or smaller will link your quilt to tradition.

GETTING THE HEIRLOOM LOOK

51

Simple Shapes—
Super Effects!

B asic geometric shapes such as circles, squares, and diamonds can yield a wide array of quilting designs, ranging from casual and simple to complex and elegant, or even whimsical. To create quilting designs from simple shapes, all you need are a few easily accessible tools and some elementary drawing skills. Arranging and manipulating these shapes in various ways will enable you to create a fresh, artistic look using classic shapes.

Getting Ready

Find a large table or other space to serve as a work surface. Use a metal yardstick for laying out long designs for borders and a compass for drawing circles. (The kind with a crossbar that holds a consistent radius is best.) If you don't have a compass, you can also use round objects such as cans, plates, bowls, or glasses as templates for circular designs. Use plain white paper for sketching or drawing small quilting motifs and freezer paper for larger designs, such as borders.

Computer design programs are an alternative to drafting designs manually. You'll need a drawing program such as Corel Draw, a printer, paper, and access to a photocopier that can enlarge and reduce designs. Using a computer will substantially speed up the process and give you many creative options.

What You'll Need

1 × 12-inch acrylic ruler

12-inch-square acrylic ruler

Yardstick

Compass or round templates

Pencils and erasers

Drawing paper

Freezer paper

Template plastic

Fine-point, permanent marker

Craft scissors for template plastic

Fabric-marking pencils

From All Angles

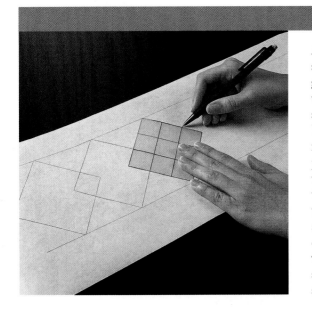

Interlocked Squares

A square divided into nine smaller squares (like a Nine Patch) makes a good guide for overlapping to create the Interlocked Squares quilting design. This linear design is great for borders, sashings, or other long, narrow spaces. Make a square template from template plastic and draw the inner grid of squares on it. Position the template at a 45-degree angle to create a horizontal row of linked squares on point. Trace around the entire square, **then move the template to one side so that one smaller square overlaps the first larger square, as shown.**

Use a square acrylic ruler with 45-degree angle lines to help you determine the size of the square template you'll need for your quilt.

Interwoven Blocks

The template for this design is the same nine-block square shape used in Interlocked Squares on page 53, but with the center square cut out. Place the template on point in a linear area. Trace around the center square. **Mark around the top left and bottom right edges. Mark the remaining two sides, skipping the upper square on the lower left side and the lower square on the top right side.** See the diagram on page 58. Move the template so that one small square overlaps the previous square, and continue marking in the same manner.

Cross Fill

Tip

Making two or three duplicate templates will allow you to arrange the repeats and to preview or check your spacing.

Another design option using squares is to make a template that omits the four corner sections of the nine-patch grid. This will allow you to create a design like Cross Fill for background areas. Trace around the template, then **offset the template to match two corners of your traced design. This tessellated design can be traced on the diagonal, creating Xs,** or straight up and down, making pluses. Rows can be straight or diagonal. See the Cross Fill pattern on page 58.

Arrowhead Border

Tip

You can use this same template and method to create a filler design for backgrounds. See page 58 for the Arrowhead Fill.

To make a versatile kite template, start out with a nine-patch square. (Refer to the "Making the Arrowhead Template" diagrams on page 58.) Draw a line from one corner to the opposite side where the first grid line meets the edge. Repeat on the other side, and cut off the triangular shapes to make the kite shape. For an Arrowhead border design, **position the long edges of the template along the border area, and trace a repeat of triangles.** Turn the template upside down, **align the short edges under each marked triangle, and trace this angle.**

54

Curves Ahead

Pumpkin Seed

Mark a circle on template plastic, and cut it out carefully. For ease in matching, draw spokes across the circle to divide it into eight equal sections. **To create a Pumpkin Seed design, mark circles in two overlapping rows to form quartets of petal or seed shapes.** To make a circle template for a Four Patch design, measure one of the squares in the Four Patch. Make the radius of your circle just slightly less than that to allow space for your tracing lines.

See page 59 for the Wineglass Fill, plus an easy Pumpkin Seed Border.

Double Pumpkin Seed Border

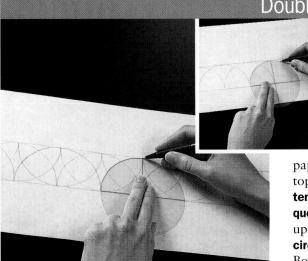

Use a circle template with a radius equal to your finished border width. Draw lines through the center to use when positioning the template. Align the diameter along the bottom edge of your border or freezer paper pattern, and mark around the top half of the template. **Move the template a half-circle for each subsequent repeat.** Then turn your work upside down and **mark the half-circles as before.** See "Pumpkin Seed Borders" on page 59.

For extra detail, add a small circle to the center area of two intersecting pumpkin seeds. (See page 59.)

Ellipses

Making the Template

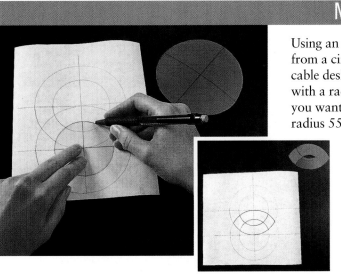

Using an ellipse, which is created from a circle, you can create many cable designs. Start with one circle with a radius the width of the space you want to fill and another with a radius 55 percent of the larger circle. **Trace around the circles, overlapping them, as shown.** The space they share is elliptical. Trace the shape onto template plastic, and **cut out the ellipse template, including the center opening.**

SIMPLE SHAPES—SUPER EFFECTS!

Cable Twist Border

One common use for the Ellipse template is this Cable Twist Border design. The design follows a straight line (this might correspond to the center of a border or a seam line on your quilt top). It features a single template repeat; the elliptical template overlaps the previous shape, using the center ellipse lines as the placement guide. **To create the twisted cable effect, mark only two outside curves of the template, omitting the corner sections.** Also trace the interior ellipse.

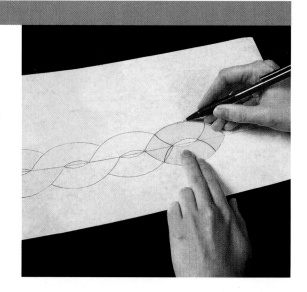

Pearl-and-Square Border

Tip

Use a hera marker and a long see-through ruler to mark the center line for the Pearl-and-Square border.

Use this design in long, narrow areas, like sashings, inner borders, or outer borders. Experiment and draw some sample Pearl-and-Square Borders to decide on the amount of overlap that appeals to you. Then mark a placement line lengthwise along the template to correspond with the center of the area to be marked. **Position the template, matching the placement line with the center of your space. Flip the template and mark each curve successively.** Refer to page 59 for variations on this design.

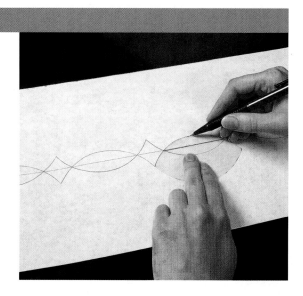

Free-Form Designs

Making a Template

You can use many simple objects or line drawings to create contemporary or innovative designs from simple shapes. A free-form petal is a good example and can serve as the basis for many exciting patterns. To create your own template, simply cut an interesting shape from a folded sheet of paper. Unfold the shape, trace it onto template plastic, and cut it out. **Mark horizontal lines across the template to use as guidelines.** This will help in creating combinations of shapes for quilting designs.

Petal Border

With the free-form petal template, you can create an interesting design like this Petal Border simply by alternating the template along a central line. First place the template so it points up, then so it points down. To line up your templates, place a guideline along the center of the horizontal design area you want to fill. **Each time you trace around the petal template, begin and end at this center line.**

Tip

You can expand this Petal Border into a fill design for blocks or background areas by repeating it in lined-up rows (see page 58).

Isolated Motifs

You can use simple shapes to create isolated motifs for plain blocks or backgrounds. Rotate a free-form petal template around a center point for a design with three to eight axes. **To fill an equilateral triangle, rotate the template 120 degrees and trace it three times. To fill a half-square triangle, rotate the template 90 degrees in three directions.** Make adaptations as necessary, by adding additional elements or using incomplete repeats to fill the space.

Creative Variations

Any free-form template you cut can be used to create beautiful quilting designs. You can rotate the template with any edge or point of the template touching the rotation point, **or move the template out from the center and add another design element, such as a circle.** All of the designs shown are based on a 90-degree rotation of the same shape, yet they all look completely different! Play around with lots of possibilities before you **zero in on the most effective quilting design for your quilt.**

SIMPLE SHAPES—SUPER EFFECTS!

Square Border

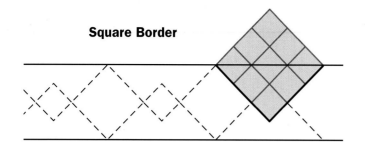

Making the Arrowhead Template

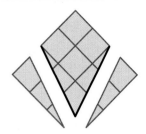
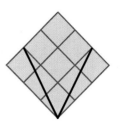

Interwoven Blocks

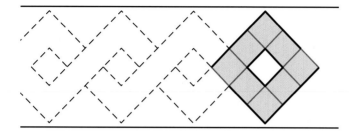

Arrowhead Fill

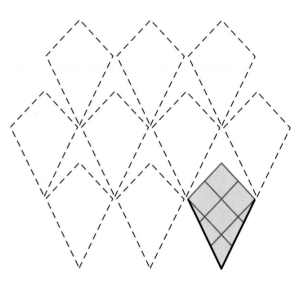

**Quilting Designs
from Simple Shapes**

Cross Border

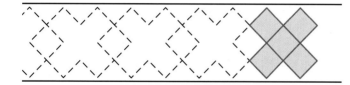

Petal Fill

Cross Fill

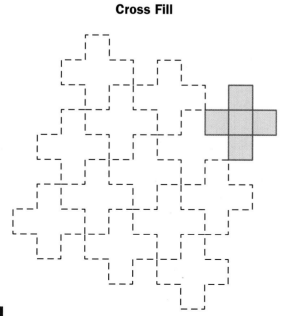

Wineglass Fill

Pumpkin Seed Borders

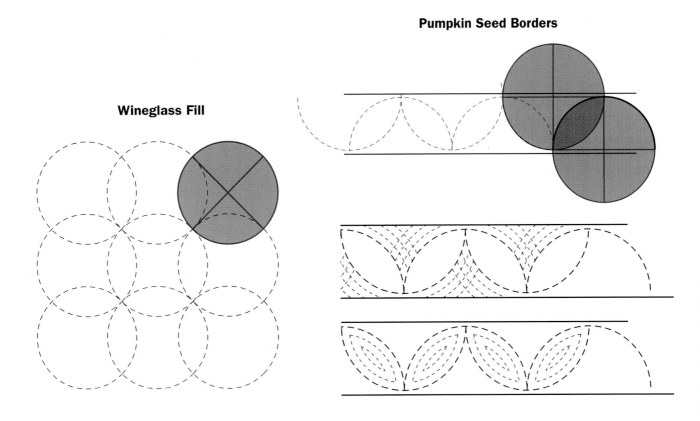

Double Pumpkin Seed Border with Circle Centers

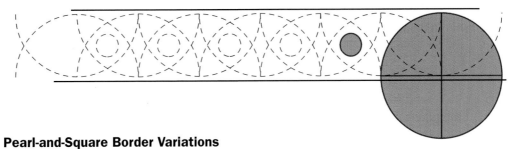

Pearl-and-Square Border Variations

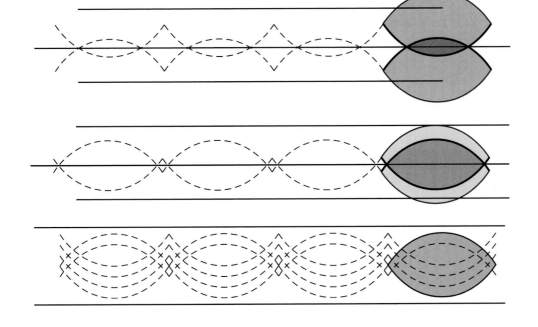

Doodling *Around*

Do you doodle while you're talking on the telephone? To add a whimsical, funky look to your machine-quilted projects, try doodle quilting! These free-motion, continuous-line motifs are fast and fun to "draw" with your sewing machine needle. Don't expect to copy the following examples exactly—like doodling with a pen or pencil, each doodle design you quilt will be intuitive, random, and as individual as your signature. Learning these distinctive loops and swirls will help you start spinning oodles of doodles!

Getting Ready

What You'll Need

- **Sewing machine**
- **Practice quilt sandwich**
- **Darning foot**
- **Machine needles (point code H-Q for machine quilting)**
- **Thread in desired color**
- **Clear nylon thread (optional)**
- **Thread snips or embroidery scissors**

Quilt artist Ami Simms insists that doodle quilting is not rocket science! In this free-form, casual type of quilting, the overall look is more important than each individual quilting stitch or motif. Try spending a bit of time stitching on a practice quilt sandwich before you begin working on your finished quilt top. Layer any size square of top fabric you like with same-size squares of batting and backing fabric, and safety pin the layers together. Set your sewing machine up for free-motion quilting by putting on a darning foot and dropping or covering the feed dogs. Begin to practice loops and swirls, stitching slowly, as you learn to coordinate the movement of the quilt with the speed of the needle. The quilts in this chapter show quilting threads in high-contrast colors, but you may want to consider using a matching color or clear nylon thread for your first quilt.

Whimsy in Thread

Squiggles

Squiggles are an overall pattern that you can use to create a heavily quilted look with very little effort. They are great for filling a patch, block, or border quickly and easily. **The object of doing freeform squiggle quilting is to purposely quilt loops that go back on themselves over and over again.** When you do this kind of quilting, think of bouclé yarn, Christmas tree lights that "got away from you," or a telephone cord gone berserk. The bee fabric in this quilt inspired this squiggle quilting design; it looks almost as if the sewing machine needle followed the flight path taken by the bumblebees.

Waves

Try filling small areas, such as patches within blocks, with a curvy path of waves. The smaller the area, the easier it is to control this doodle pattern. **If the patches in your quilt blocks line up diagonally, as in this quilt, don't start and stop at each corner. Instead, move from one patch to the other diagonally.** Remember—there is no right or wrong way to doodle quilt!

Crossing Waves

Sashing strips get a face-lift with gently undulating doodles. Once you establish your own rhythm, these doodles just flow. Proceed from one end of a sashing strip to another, working along all the vertical strips, then all the horizontal strips. If there are corner squares in the sashing arrangement, cross them with straight, diagonal lines that move from corner to corner. Do just a little planning ahead for these doodles, so that **when the quilting is complete, you will have a crisp X through each of the setting squares.**

Loops

Another easy doodle is this large looping pattern, which resembles handwriting exercises often done in grade school. This motif quilts up fast, so stitching this design a few times on a practice quilt sandwich is probably all you'll need to get the feel of the pattern before you're ready to stitch the real thing on your quilt.

Loop de Loops

Borders are the perfect place to doodle quilt loopy designs. This one is easy to quilt randomly after doing a dry run on a practice quilt sandwich. You can also mark it on your quilt top with a chalk pencil, if you like the security of planning and spacing the loops. For the smoothest, most graceful loops, keep up a free-flowing rhythm for each loop and each curve between loops. If you want or need to stop, do so at the base of the loop, where the stitching lines intersect, and set the needle of the machine to stop in the down position.

Tip

Treat all four corners of a quilt in a similar fashion, or quilt a different pattern of loops at each corner.

Coils

Quilting coils of concentric shapes is a great way to stitch an overall quilting design on a single patch or block. **Let circles, squares, ovals, or triangles spiral inward or outward randomly as you stitch.** Put lots of space in between them, or hardly any—it's your choice! The only drawback to this design is that you need to start and stop lines of stitching for each area to avoid stitching a connecting line through the coil.

Tip

To begin or end a doodle, take three small stitches in place. Afterward, clip the thread ends close to the surface.

Script

Your own handwriting is one of the most personal touches you can add to any quilt. **With doodle quilting, you can sign your name or quilt a message right on your quilt.** Cursive handwriting can be tough to do free-form, without lots of practice, so it can be helpful to plot out your message on paper that is the same size as the intended border area. That way, you can practice your "penmanship" ahead of time, making sure that your message will link both letters and words for a continuous flow of text.

Tip

Remember to cross your t's as you are writing them. A few tight stitches in one place will dot your i's later.

DOODLING AROUND

Fun, Fresh & Free-Motion

Once you have mastered the art of free-motion quilting, the range of continuous-line patterns you can choose for your quilts will be endless. You'll enjoy the freedom of being able to stitch in all directions. Practice the fanciful, fun, continuous-line quilting designs in this chapter, then dream up some additional patterns of your own to add interesting effects and texture to your quilts.

Getting Ready

What You'll Need

- **Sewing machine**
- **Darning foot**
- **Practice quilt sandwiches**
- **Thread for machine quilting**
- **Scissors**

Before quilting any type of free-motion quilting design, you'll need to set up your sewing machine properly. Lower or cover the feed dogs, attach a darning or free-motion foot to your machine, and loosen the tension. Be sure to practice on a quilt sandwich to find the right tension for your machine and the right speed to move your quilt through your machine so you'll get a fairly consistent stitch length. If you are not already comfortable with the basics of free-motion quilting techniques (such as stippling and meander quilting), take time to practice those first. Photocopy the designs on pages 70 and 71, and enlarge them 150 to 300 percent on separate sheets of paper. Use an unthreaded machine needle to stitch along the lines until you feel familiar with the free-motion stitching process. With time, you'll become proficient enough to work these designs in smaller scale. If you want additional guidance, take a machine-quilting workshop or class at your local quilt shop, where you can enjoy the benefits of a skilled instructor.

Continuous-Line Designs

Horizontal Hearts

You can stitch Horizontal Hearts nestled together to create a band with scalloped edges, or as a line of "loop-de-loops" with space between the hearts. Stitched in a single straight line, these hearts are perfect for sashings or borders, or you might quilt them in rows as an overall design. With practice, you could go a step further and work these hearts in curved lines, filling background areas around appliqués or superimposing a sweet, wavy pattern over patchwork.

Tip

To test a new quilting design for continuous-line stitching potential, see if you can draw the design on paper without lifting your pencil.

FUN, FRESH & FREE-MOTION

65

Vertical Hearts

Vertical hearts look great along a seam line or in a narrow sashing strip, bar, or border. Stitch one half of each heart in a continuous line for the length of the border, and then go back up and finish the other side of each heart.

Square Stippling

Square stipple quilting is a pattern that can be somewhat difficult to master, but **it is an innovative twist on regular curved stippling because of its angular edges.** Spend some time stitching on a practice quilt sandwich to master these squared points. Work back and forth, from side to side or vertically, to fill a space with angular stippling lines that do not cross each other.

Broken Stars

These little broken stars are fun to quilt on pieced star quilts or to stitch in the sky area of a landscape quilt. **Begin by "drawing" a basic five-pointed star with your machine needle, but don't complete the last point.** Instead, continue from the tip of the star point into the adjacent space and create another broken five-pointed star. The result will be stars that are easier to space.

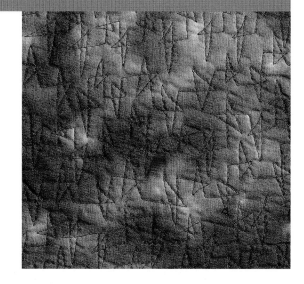

Laura's Leaf

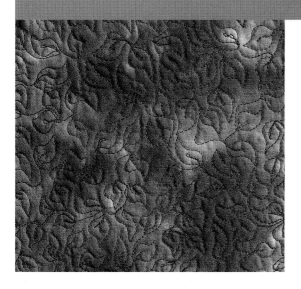

Connect leaves with viney stems for a fast and easy free-motion quilting pattern. Make the outline of the leaf first, come about halfway up the middle to make the vein, and then move on to the next leaf. **This leaf pattern is great for covering large expanses of space quickly.**

Folk Art Forest

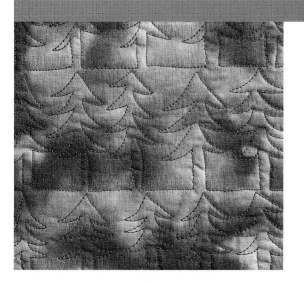

While this rustic repeat design works handsomely as an overall pattern, just one row of Folk Art Forest is a great design for borders. **Start at the bottom of a tree, stitch the trunk, "branch" out on one side of the tree, and keep going until your tree is as tall as you wish.** Then work your way back down the other side of the tree, connecting it to the next tree by stitching a line that indicates the ground. You'll come up with variations on this theme: an orchard of deciduous trees, a border garden of simple zinnias or sunflowers, or a row of snowmen!

Seaweed

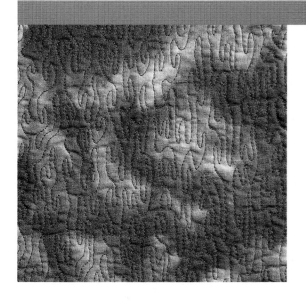

For an allover design that looks great in water-theme quilt designs or for adding texture to a quilt that needs a little life, choose the pattern shown here. Think of long, pulled-apart stipple quilting. **If the lines are mostly vertical, it gives the impression of seaweed.** Turn the pattern horizontally and work it over a cool blue-green fabric, and you'll find the perfect texture for calm waters.

Tip

Change the direction of the Seaweed pattern in different areas of the same quilt.

FUN, FRESH & FREE-MOTION

67

Folky Flowers

These whimsical little flowers are perfect for quilting folk art and floral quilts. Give the flowers any number of petals you like—four to six petals, or whatever works best for the space that you wish to fill in your quilt. Experiment by connecting the flowers with wavy stems in different lengths until you create a design that appeals to you.

Spirals

Contemporary quilts are a wonderful place to feature machine-quilted spirals. **Avoid crossing a line of stitching: Make back and forth arcs,** or make your curved lines far enough apart so that when you reach the center of the curl there's still room to spiral back out. When you're finished stitching one spiral, "squiggle" on over to where you want to place the next center spiral, and continue in the same manner. It's best to aim for random placements, rather than trying to achieve uniformity.

Interesting Echo

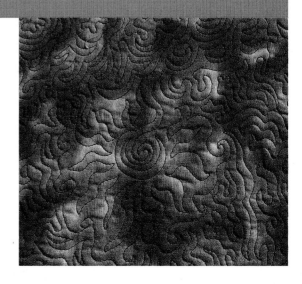

This pattern is more complex and does require practice. You'll need to feel confident in your ability to fill spaces and achieve a nice balance of density. However, once mastered, this design will add a great deal of visual interest to almost any quilt with large, unpieced areas. **Start with a basic pattern that you like, such as Spirals, and then surround that pattern with lines of echo quilting and random machine stippling.** Use curves for a calm look, spikey lines for excitement, or a combination of the two for a truly unique design.

The Quilter's
Problem Solver

Stress & Tension

Problem	Solution
You have to get your quilt finished in a hurry: which quilting design should you choose?	Choose any free-motion, continuous-line design that you enjoy stitching and that does not require a lot of dense quilting in small areas. And suit the theme of your chosen design to the theme or style of your quilt. The Seaweed pattern in this chapter would be great for a fish quilt, while the Folky Flowers design would complement a floral quilt top. You can also combine designs in one quilt, as long as you keep the size of the quilting motifs and the distance of open space between the quilting lines consistent.
Tension problems plague your free-motion quilting.	Analyze what you see happening on your quilt. If your top tension is too loose, you will see loops on the bottom of your quilt. If the top tension is too tight, you'll notice bobbin thread or "spider legs" on the top of your quilt. You can correct for improper tension by remembering this simple rule—the higher the number on your machine setting, the tighter the tension, and the lower the number, the looser the tension. You'll rarely need to adjust the lower bobbin thread tension, but if that is necessary, you can insert a small screwdriver (the one that came with your sewing machine) into the larger screw on the thread tension spring and turn it slightly, no more than $\frac{1}{16}$-inch at a time. Which way do you turn it? Just remember this phrase: "righty, tighty—lefty, loosey," and you won't go wrong. You might want to keep a separate, marked, tension-adjusted bobbin case solely for free-motion stitching.

Skill Builder

Cut the fingers from a pair of quilter's gloves to provide more control.

Snip the fingertips off all the fingers on a pair of quilter's gloves, and wear these fingerless gloves when you are free-motion quilting. You'll gain the benefit of using the fabric of the gloves to help your palms control and manipulate a quilt more easily, and you'll still be able to remove pins, rethread your sewing machine needle, and capture stray threads with your bare fingers.

Try This!

Make use of interesting backing fabric for creative background quilting designs.

Select a backing fabric with a pattern that lends itself to being followed as a quilting pattern. Begin by quilting isolated motifs or other designs while working from the front of the quilt, then turn the quilt over and fill the background areas with quilting that follows the lines of the interesting print fabric you've used as a backing. Use a decorative thread in the bobbin (which will show up well on your quilt front), and allow the pattern to take shape randomly on the front as you quilt from the reverse side.

FUN, FRESH & FREE-MOTION

Square Stippling

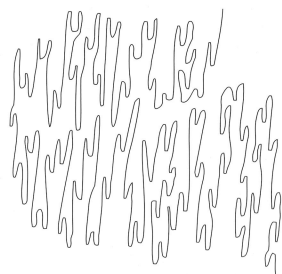

Seaweed

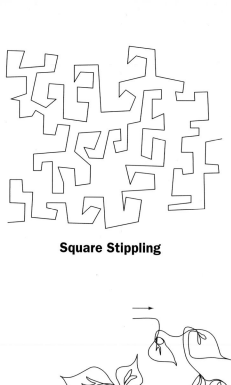

Laura's Leaf

**Reduced Patterns
for Free-Motion
Quilting Designs**
by Laura Heine

Vertical Spirals

Spirals

Broken Stars

Vertical Hearts

Folky Flowers

Interesting Echo

Folk Art Forest

Horizontal Hearts

Fanciful *Feathers*

F eathers are one of the most popular of all quilting designs and, believe it or not, one of the easiest to draw yourself! Designing your own feathered quilting patterns is one of the best ways to guarantee that your designs will fit specific areas of your quilt, no matter how large, how small, or what shape those areas may be. Using a handy new design template, Infinite Feathers, you can create feathers that will grace your quilts with elegance and style.

Getting Ready

Start by doing a bit of research into feathered designs. Look at books, photos, and quilts that feature all sorts of different feathered wreaths, isolated motifs, and continuous-line feathered designs. Notice how and where these designs are used in quilts. Think about the kinds of quilts you like to make and where you can incorporate the same or similar designs. Drawing feathered quilting designs as shown in this chapter will be easy using the Infinite Feathers design template from Anita Shackelford. This tool allows you to preview the placement of each feather and to repeat the same feather shape as many times as you like. Check your local quilt shop for this helpful design tool, or see "Resources" on page 126 to order it by mail.

Quilt top, ready for marking

Infinite Feathers quilting design template

Mechanical pencil

Paper

Compass or a circle stencil

Protractor

Freezer paper

Washable graphite pencil

Acrylic ruler

Eraser

Fine-point, permanent marker

Masking tape

Straight pins

Feathered Wreaths

To draft a feathered wreath for a specific-size block, draw two perpendicular lines, dividing the space into four quarters. **Use a circle stencil to add a center circle** in whatever size you want to use for your feathered wreath. This example shows a 2-inch circle for a 7-inch square block, making the circle about one-third the size of the space that the quilting design should fill.

Use a protractor to **add radiating lines at 45 degree angles or closer,** depending on the number of feathers you want in your design. You will use these as placement lines.

2

Choose a feather size on the Infinite Feathers tool in the desired length for your design and a little wider than the distance between radiating lines, to provide a slight overlap. Position the template over one radiating line, with the narrow tip of the feather touching the center circle. Play with angles to determine the look you want. Draw the outside curve of the feather. **Use a washable graphite pencil to trace the placement line onto the tool, above and below the feather shape. Your first marked feather should resemble a half-teardrop shape.**

3

Tip

Trace over your final design on freezer paper, using a fine-point, black permanent marker.

Match your marked lines on the Infinite Feathers tool to an adjacent placement line, positioning the tip of the feather shape on the circle. Draw the curve as before. **Draw the outer curves of successive feathers in the same way. Continue until your feathered wreath pattern is complete.** For wreaths with feathers on the inside of a circle as well as the outside, the process is much the same. Use every other or every third placement line in this smaller space.

Versatile Proportions

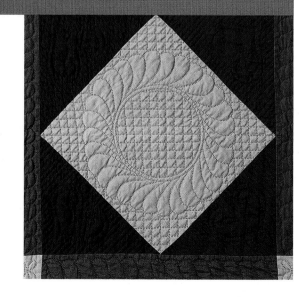

Tip

Keep an artist's circle template on hand for drawing centers for feathered wreaths in a variety of different sizes.

Circular feathered wreaths are a good choice to fill a square space, such as a center medallion or alternate plain blocks. Although a feathered wreath should fill the block to within ½ inch of the seam lines, there are many variations for sizing the wreath center and feather size. You can use a small or large center circle with feathers that are similar or different in scale. Also consider single or double veins around the center circle and feathers on the inside. Fill the interior and exterior areas with crosshatch grid quilting, if desired.

FANCIFUL FEATHERS

Squared Off

Another option for a square area such as a plain block is a modified, squared, feathered wreath. Draw diagonal placement lines across the square you want to fill. Add a center circle and as many radiating placement lines as the number of feathers you want, using a protractor. Draw a square ½ inch inside the edges of the square. Mark the feather shapes as before, keeping the top curve of each feather you mark along this boundary and centering a larger feather along each corner diagonal.

To create the 5-inch-square design shown, start with a 2-inch-center circle. Use Infinite Feathers guide #3 along each side, #7 at each corner.

Fitting Other Shapes

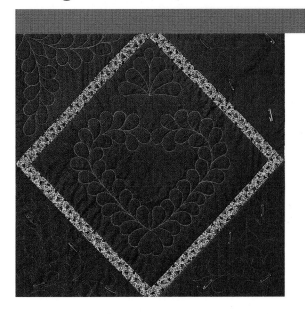

On-Point Blocks

When a quilt includes blocks set on-point, a heart-shape feathered wreath may be the perfect choice. **The heart shape stands upright, with the lower point at the bottom corner.** Enlarge the pattern for the heart-shape feather wreath on page 79, or simply refer to it to draft your own design. To create a beautiful heart shape, fold tracing paper in half, draw half a heart along the fold, and cut the complete shape. Use the Infinite Feathers tool to space feathers evenly along one side, then trace them onto the other side.

Consider adding a small, pyramidal feathered motif to fill the top corner of a feathered heart in a square on-point.

Rectangles

To fill a rectangular space, consider feathers around a center shape that has the same proportions. **When the length of your space is just a bit larger than the width, a central teardrop or pineapple shape works better than a circle.** Begin with a center shape that is approximately one-third of the size of the block. Add feathers around one side, then fold and trace the already-marked feathers along the other side. Refine your design: Adapt feather sizes to fill the space, or add background quilting to complement the feathered motif.

Use a Clamshell quilting pattern to fill the center area of a feathered pineapple.

FANCIFUL FEATHERS

75

Triangles

Drawing a feathered design to fit a triangular area is usually more effective than simply cutting a full block pattern in half diagonally. **Single symmetrical shapes, such as these sprays or peacock feathers, can be used to fill small triangular spaces.** Experiment by drawing curved lines on folded freezer paper to create symmetrical vein shapes of your own. For more complexity, add a double vein, more spines, and offshoots of feathers that flow into each corner of a triangular area.

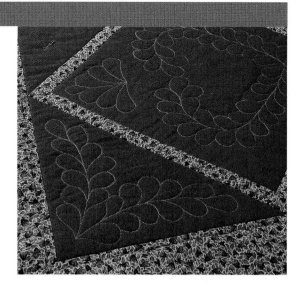

Whimsies for Backgrounds

Tip

Flip a feathers template to create the two mirror-image sides of a heart shape.

Open background areas sometimes benefit from the addition of fancy little feathered motifs. This is a good place to use motifs that might not fill a standard block. **Symmetrical combinations of feathers in flower shapes or asymmetrical combinations of plumes bring charm to open spaces behind appliqué designs.** After quilting these individual designs, fill in the background with smaller-scale crosshatching or other filler quilting.

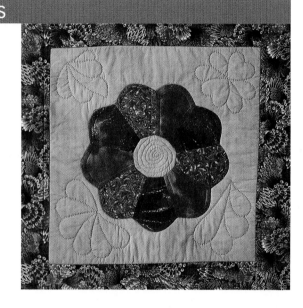

Feathers on Top

You may never have thought of using feathered motifs in areas other than wholecloth or open backgrounds, but they can also be very effective when they are quilted right over the top of other designs. **Consider feathers running across patchwork, such as a large, unfurling plume quilted over each arm of a Lone Star.** Feathers can also add texture and detail when quilted inside appliqué shapes, such as a small, feathered wreath inside a flower.

Feathers for Borders

Undulating Designs

Feathered swags or **running feathers add a feeling of movement and create a graceful frame in the borders of a quilt.** Draw feather shapes along an undulating line by eye, and experiment to achieve the best spacing. Feather shapes on an outer curve should stand up straighter than those along an inner curve, and you can usually fit more of them on outer curves. Undulations will leave open areas that are best filled with additional background quilting, such as a chevron design, diagonal lines, or stipple quilting.

Tip

Feathers quilted on a straight spine can fill border spaces completely without the need for background quilting.

Continuous Corners

Plan smooth undulating feathered designs around the corners of a border. Work out the entire border design on perpendicular sheets of freezer paper that correspond to one quarter of the border, including a corner. Trace repeats of running feathers so that the undulations end on a downswing at each corner. Draft the center spine of the curve needed to fill the corner, matching the ends to the border repeats. Your drawn curve will invariably be broader or tighter than your border repeat; use the repeat as a guide, making adjustments.

Broken Corners

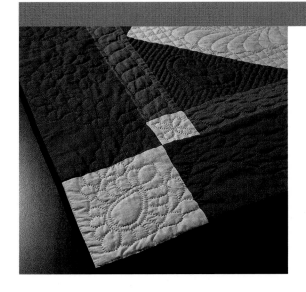

A simpler alternative to making a feathered design turn a corner is to simply break the flow of the design with a completely different motif. You don't need a contrast fabric corner square to break the design, but if you have one, all the more reason to insert an isolated, feathered motif. Keep the feathers of your corner motif in scale with those in the feathered border and strive to have the designs flow into one another. **The feathered garlands in this border are a natural extension of the feathered teardrop motif in the corner.**

FANCIFUL FEATHERS

**Quilting Designs
for Feathers**
by Anita Shackelford

Enlarge the patterns on these pages
as needed, and alter the proportions
by using more or fewer and larger or
smaller feathers.

Picture-Perfect *Details*

Picture this: quilting stitches that enhance the realistic images in your quilts. Whether you like to make patchwork or appliqué quilts with a contemporary, folk art, or traditional feel, the lines of your quilting stitches can make a real difference in the overall effect in the finished quilt. You'll be adding visual interest, texture, and dimension that will make your quilt a true work of art.

Getting Ready

What You'll Need

Pictorial or other appropriate quilt top

Marking pencils for marking quilting designs

Threads for machine or hand quilting

Sewing machine

Hand needles

Sewing supplies

To create pictorial quilting designs, look at line art, coloring books, cartoons, artist's sketches, or pen and ink drawings. Notice the impact and detail that quilted lines can add to shapes. Think about the types of lines you can create with quilting stitches and thread choices. If you want a thick, solid line, consider using thread as thick as your machine will accommodate on top. Heavier lines may be created by couching a decorative thread simultaneously while you quilt; perhaps you might use thicker threads in the bobbin and work from the back of the quilt. For broken lines, short or long dashed lines, and delicate details, hand quilting will probably work best.

If you are in the early stages of making a quilt, and especially if you lack confidence in your drawing abilities, check your stash and your local quilt shop for pictorial fabrics. Whenever you find clear outlines and other details, you know it will be easy to quilt along the printed features.

Focus on the Details

Wood & Stone

Quilting can provide wonderful, natural texture. In the quilt on the opposite page, notice the straight-line quilting in the clapboards on the house and the texture of the dirt path leading down to the foreground. **In the quilt shown here, the rough grain of the birdhouse and the fence post are also rendered in quilting stitches.** While there are pictorial fabrics for wood and stone, with quilting you add texture and quilting stitches provide depth, dimension, and shadow.

Natural Surfaces

The rims of clay pots and the outer layer of boards on the wooden shutter in this quilt are brought out and visually enhanced by quilting. As your stitches depress the fabric, they create a sense of the planes, the roundness, and the dimension of the portrayed objects as they exist in reality.

Skies, Wind & Movement

Tip

To machine-quilt clouds, consider white, pastel, variegated, rayon, or silvery metallic threads.

You can enhance the sky in a landscape quilt by quilting fluffy clouds or swirling winds. Horizontal meandering lines of quilting can suggest wispy clouds. Hand-quilt gentle drops, or machine-stitch pelting rain and a crack of lightning.

Your quilting stitches can also add a sense of movement (like the flutter of butterfly wings) or a sense of perspective (as from lines that come together along a horizon or in the distance).

Watery Effects

Tip

For a whimsical folk art look, add high, scalloping waves to the background of a sailboat block.

For a scene that includes a pool, pond, lake, stream, river, ocean, or waterfall, you can add a flowing feel with your quilting. **Water that laps the shoreline ripples in gentle curves following the contour of a pieced or appliquéd shore. Free-motion machine quilting is the perfect way to achieve this effect.**

When stones or fish create a disturbance on the surface of water, concentric circles appear. To achieve this look, quilt concentric circles, making them oval, wavy, and spaced farther apart as they widen out.

Foliage

There's nothing like a fine line of quilting to create the look of a leaf vein. Use quilting to outline leaves and petals or to stitch stamens, stems, tendrils, striations of color, ridges, and other subtle, true-to-life details.

If your quilt features a clear object, such as a glass bottle, a jar, or a pair of eyeglasses, define the shape with your quilting lines.

Plumping Out a Form

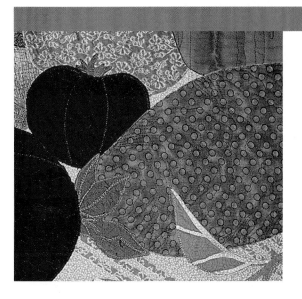

To suggest the roundness and ridges of a tomato, quilting lines produce realistic results. Outlining any appliqué with quilting will make it pop out. Use this trick to treat pumpkins on Halloween wall hangings or autumn table runners to quilted ridges and outlines. Consider using trapunto to give even more dimension to vegetables, plants, and leaves.

Animating Animals

Pieced or appliquéd designs of realistic or stylized animals are a marvelous opportunity for creative quilting. **Quilt feathers and wings on birds** or scales and fins on fish. Quilt facial elements such as noses and lips or wrinkles and dimples on people. Quilt hair, fur, and whiskers on cats and dogs or creatures of the wild.

PICTURE-PERFECT DETAILS

Folk Art
Charm

Folk art is literally art that is created by people, just like you and me, without a professional background in design or a degree in art. Pioneer quilters, who did not have access to fancy quilting templates, stencils, or commercial patterns, used whatever they had on hand. But even with all the currently available patterns and tools, we all recognize the strong emotional appeal of simple, homey designs. Read on to see how you can add the endearing charm of folk art to your quilting.

Getting Ready

When it comes to sources of inspiration for folk art quilting designs, consider many of the quilts from the last half of the nineteenth century. These beautiful quilts were often made from richly colored calicoes with simple, graphic patchwork and appliqué designs. The quilting designs were usually both utilitarian and creative. To find contemporary counterparts of these designs, you won't have to look far. There are likely to be plenty of sources right in your own home. Take some time to go exploring—look through your kitchen cabinets, check out your pantry shelves, closets, and junk drawers. You'll probably be surprised at the sources you find for charming quilting designs. For other ideas, turn to "Great Inspirations" on page 42. Just keep in mind that the simpler and more informal the designs you choose, the more your quilts will have the feel of folk art.

For other ideas, turn to "Great Inspirations" on page 42.

What You'll Need

- **Assortment of everyday objects**
- **Pencils and paper**
- **Tracing paper**
- **Freezer paper or template plastic**
- **Marking tools of your choice**

All Around the House

Baking Tools

Your favorite dessert and baking tools can become whimsical folk art quilting designs. **Cookie cutters are naturals for creating quilting designs in a wide variety of shapes.** And don't ignore the possibilities in gelatin and salad molds, fancy cake pans, and festive holiday serving dishes. Raid your kitchen drawers for wooden spoons, cake servers, pasta measures, even grandma's wrought-iron trivet.

Don't worry if your quilted shapes turn out lopsided after you're finished stitching—imperfections are part of the appeal of folk art, too!

FOLK ART CHARM

85

Foods for Thought

Tip

Try quilting with heavy button and carpet thread or pearl cotton and a large needle to make big, fun, folksy-looking stitches.

Sketches of fruits and vegetables make wonderful quilting designs. Don't be self-conscious about your drafting skills—remember, this is folk art! And don't forget to look in the pantry. Check the labels on jellies, jams, preserves, and canned goods for strong, clear images that you can trace, photocopy, modify, **and enlarge so that your quilting designs will fit and fill the open spaces of your quilt top.**

Teacups & Saucers

Think of all the different sizes of circles you have in your own kitchen, from egg cups and juice glasses all the way up to your best china teacups. A traditional favorite folk art quilting design called "teacup quilting" consisted of **circular designs that were made by repeatedly tracing around teacups and saucers. These fairly random circles give a whimsical flair to the border of a retro-style quilt with a repeat Teacup block,** but they would be just as suitable in a really contemporary quilt.

Sewing Tools

Tip

Quilt the outline of a spool and add a meandering line of stitches to create the look of thread unwinding from it.

Some design sources are near and dear to the heart of every quilter, and right in your sewing room. Think about tracing, sketching, and incorporating tools such as scissors or shears, spools of every size, thimbles, pincushions, rulers, sewing baskets, bobbins, and more. **Play around with these motifs in different arrangements to suit the open spaces in your quilt.** Adapt the designs shown here and on pages 88 and 89, substituting your own favorite sewing tools.

FOLK ART CHARM

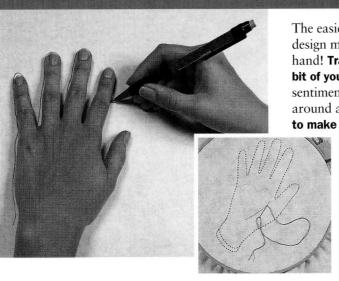

The easiest, most personal quilting design may be as close as your own hand! **Trace around your hand to put a bit of yourself into your work.** For a sentimental finishing touch, trace around a heart-shaped cookie cutter **to make the classic heart-in-hand, a traditional folk art motif.** You might also quilt your name or initials inside the heart. Are you making a child's quilt or a special gift for Mother's Day? Trace around a child's hand, and use that as your repeat quilting motif.

Tip

Use the hand motif with your name and date for adding a special label to your quilt.

Supplied by Mother Nature

Leaves

Collect interesting leaves such as maple, oak, gingko, or tulip tree leaves. Lay the leaves over open spaces of your quilt top and trace around them, then **quilt the leaf outline, adding veins freehand.** Take the folk art approach where designs are simple interpretations, and don't worry about whether they look like real leaves.

Flowers

Draw a few daisies freehand. Simple shapes like single posies are pretty for filling in open areas on a quilt, while a daisy chain might make a perfect border design. **Sketching from a window on a summer day inspired the wholecloth design shown here.** Lines of diagonal quilting stitches frame the scene and play up the casual feeling.

Tip

Use pressed flowers from a bride's bouquet to create floral quilting designs for an anniversary quilt.

FOLK ART CHARM

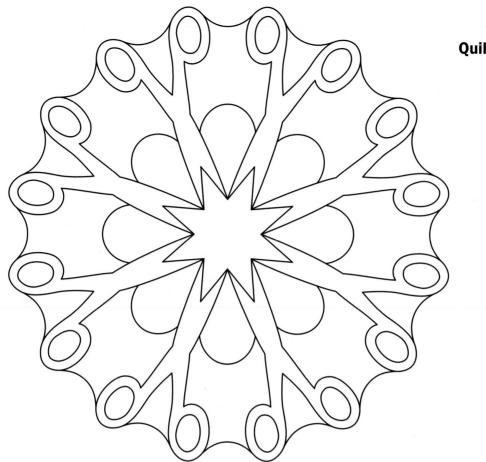

**Folk Art
Quilting Designs**

**Scissors and Spools
Designs**
by Diane Rode Schneck

FOLK ART CHARM

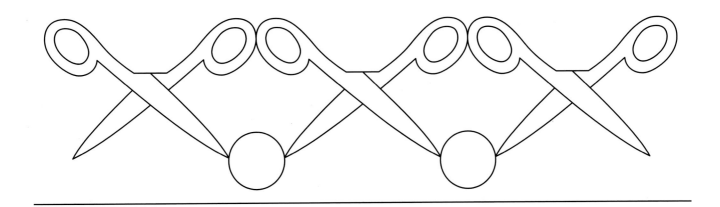

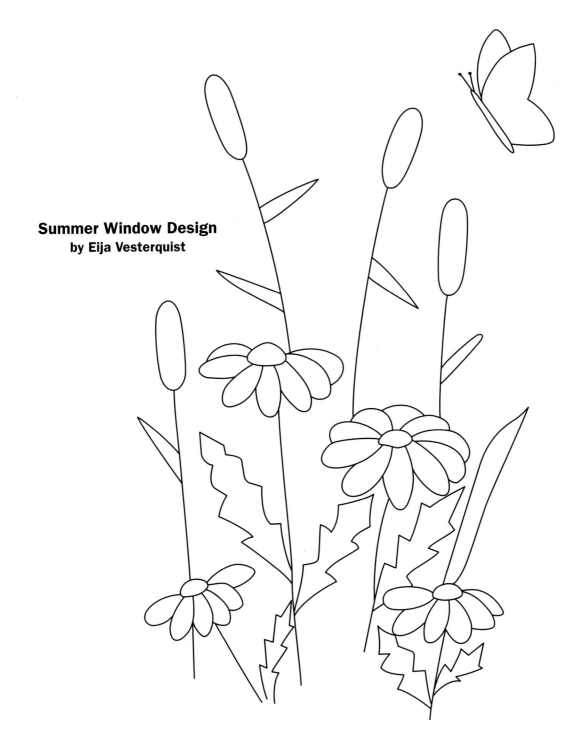

Summer Window Design
by Eija Vesterquist

African
Rhythms

African fabrics feature intense colors, bold geometric patterns, and powerful cultural symbols that have made them an instant hit with quilters everywhere. Whether printed, stamped, batik, or hand-dyed, these vibrant fabrics bring a sense of excitement to any quilt. They can also inspire many dynamic quilting designs, which may be necessary to stand up to the strength and drama of these fabrics.

Getting Ready

Time for a trip! You don't have to go as far as Africa, though. Check out the vendors at regional or national quilt shows and visit your favorite quilt shops to scout authentic African fabrics and other prints that have an African feel. Look for mud cloth from Mali, batiks (also known as adire cloth in Nigeria), and fabrics printed with African motifs such as masks, round houses, animals indigenous to Africa, and cultural symbols. Start a collection of these great fabrics, keeping an eye out for prints that would make good quilting designs. If you find yourself strongly drawn to particular fabrics, purchase small amounts of each and analyze specific elements that would make interesting quilting designs. Create a quilt or use your fabrics strictly for inspiration. Be open to this creative experience so that you can enjoy it to the fullest.

What You'll Need

African and African-inspired fabrics

Pencil

Paper or freezer paper

Cardboard

Paper scissors

Heavyweight threads

Solid-color fabrics in earth tones and black

Fabric scissors

Fabric Inspirations

Authentic & Inspired Prints

Stay on the lookout for authentic African fabrics, as well as African-inspired fabrics manufactured in America. With both of these types of fabrics, there are often different design elements going on at the same time. **For example, a background geometric pattern may have floating motifs such as masks, birds, drums, or shields superimposed on it.** You can use any or all of these elements individually to create quilting designs. Or consider a combination of geometric and pictorial quilting designs for any quilt.

AFRICAN RHYTHMS

Motifs Through a Window

Tip

You can also trace or photocopy these fabric patterns instead, then simplify or modify the design lines for quilting.

To view fabric motifs or portions of designs individually, it's helpful to make a window template. Cut two L-shaped pieces of cardboard; **overlap the ends to frame square or rectangular areas of an African print that you think may offer some interesting quilting design options.** Sketch any graphics that appeal to you on plain sheets of paper, and use these sketches to develop **quilting patterns that can add complexity and richness to your quilts.**

Mud Cloth

Tip

To give a quilt the look of African mud cloth, quilt in ivory-color, heavyweight threads on black, brown, and other earth-tone fabrics.

African mud cloth, while far heavier than quilter's cottons, features simple and strong repeat patterns that can inspire many quilting designs for blocks, borders, and sashing strips. Examine any fabrics you are considering; use the same window-template approach described above to isolate portions of the designs, and sketch potential candidates for quilting stitches. You may be surprised at how many different quilting designs you can derive from a single piece of this exotic fabric.

Batiks

African batiks contain motifs such as animals, leaves, and abstract patterns that are stamped or stenciled onto the fabric using wax before the fabric is dyed. The result is very simple outlined shapes. To quilt these fabrics easily, stitch directly along the design lines of individual motifs, using contrasting thread in a slightly heavier weight, such as Mettler's Jeans Stitch quilting thread or YLI's Jeans Stitch. **Fill in some extra details, such as the ear and curly tail on this elephant, and add echo quilting to emphasize the shape.**

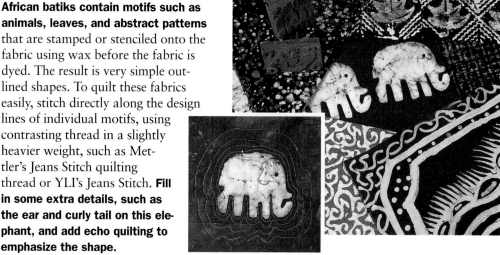

AFRICAN RHYTHMS

Showcasing African Designs

Solid Choices

To make African quilting designs the focal point of a quilt, quilt them on black, white, or ivory solid-color fabrics. Make sure that the color of the fabric is saturated enough to stand up to the strong, African-style quilting designs, and use a contrasting-color thread.

 Tip

If possible, use dark batting behind dark fabrics to prevent bearding (white batting fibers escaping through to the surface).

Backgrounds & Blocks

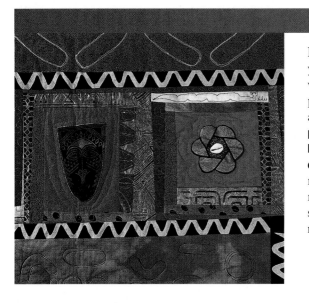

Provide balance and visual interest in your quilt with quilting designs as a way of making sure that the African prints connect and blend with quieter areas. **Echo the strong shapes of appliquéd motifs and create texture for backgrounds and plain blocks with quilting designs.** Rhythmic geometrics, even more dynamic if they are irregular or asymmetrical, will add spark to areas where there is little or no graphic interest.

Tip

Be open to intuitive creativity; your quilting designs will often tell *you* where they want to go in a quilt.

Borders & Sashing

In long, narrow borders, the simpler you keep the quilting designs, the better. Repeats of simple African designs can make a quilt look bolder and more exciting. In Africa, snakes are a cultural symbol of protection. **Use snakes as quilting designs to bring African style, grace, and mystery to long, narrow areas.**

**African-Style
Quilting Designs**
by Myrah Brown Green

Sashiko
Sensations

In the Japanese style of quilting called sashiko, highly visible lines of stitching form exciting geometrics and graceful curving designs. Traditionally done by hand in heavy white thread, these designs are easy to machine quilt. No matter what technique you use, you'll find that sashiko patterns can add interest and elegance to both traditional and contemporary quilts. The results are simply stunning when East meets West!

Getting Ready

In traditional sashiko (pronounced SAH-shee-ko), small pieces of indigo-dyed fabric were often joined together to make one larger piece of fabric. White sashiko hand stitches minimized the differences in color between the fabrics. Today, you can use sashiko designs to decorate a whole-cloth quilt or to enhance the plain areas between patches and appliqués. Consider how your favorite quilts might look with one of the quilting designs shown on these pages. With machine quilting, you can take full advantage of continuous-line sashiko patterns.

Practice making well-defined stitches using a jeans/denim needle (which has a sharp point, unlike a universal needle, which has a rounded point). Also make sure that your needle is making a large enough hole for heavier threads to penetrate. On the samples shown, a 100 needle (equivalent to a size 16) was used, along with YLI Jeans Stitch thread, the perfect weight for showcasing 3 mm (8 stitches per inch) sashiko stitches.

What You'll Need

- **Quilt top or practice sandwich**
- **Ruler**
- **Fabric marker of choice**
- **Sewing machine with size 100 needle (equivalent to a size 16)**
- **Sewing needle with a large eye**
- **YLI Jeans Stitch thread**

Simple Line Designs

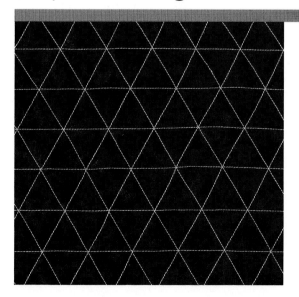

1

One simple yet effective sashiko pattern is this *Mitsu-Uroko*, or Fish Scales pattern, featuring two diagonals and one horizontal line that intersect. You can continuous-line machine quilt many straight-line sashiko designs like this one, working from one edge of a quilt to the other. Mark the lines consistently, using an acrylic ruler. Using white thread, stitch all the parallel lines that go in one direction, then stitch the lines that go in a second direction, and follow with the third set of lines. See the diagram for the Fish Scales pattern on page 100.

This quilting design called *Kagome*, or Woven Bamboo, starts with a set of two diagonals and one horizontal. Since the lines do not intersect but are offset evenly, a six-pointed star results. **For even more complexity, double the lines.** This makes a nice background or filler quilting design and would also work well for borders. See the diagram for this pattern on page 100.

3

For a sashiko look that takes little effort, you can stitch in the ditch to outline smaller blocks and patches using heavy white thread. Carry your stitching lines on to alternate plain blocks and showcase simple but direct sashiko patterns within the areas formed by the extended lines. In this sample, **the *Hirasan-Kuzushi* (Paving Blocks) design, at lower left, and *Tsumeta* (Rice Fields) design, at upper right, follow naturally from the stitched-in-the-ditch lines.**

4

Superimposing curved quilting lines, like this gently undulating *Fundo* (Counterweights) pattern, over straight-line patchwork adds a sense of movement and lightness. To mark this design, enlarge the diagram on page 100 to the size you want and trace the pattern onto your quilt top. Alternatively, follow two adjacent rows of wavy lines on the enlarged pattern to mark and cut a template strip from template material. Mark guidelines to align a set of lines in the opposite direction. Mark one set of lines, then the others; quilt in the order shown on page 100.

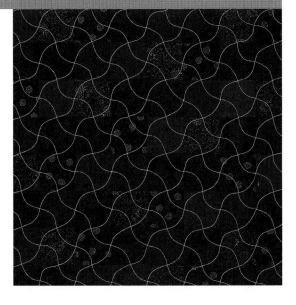

Quilting "Relatives"

Patchwork "Twins"

Some sashiko designs are identical to or similar to pieced designs and work well with the corresponding patchwork design. **Here, the sashiko *Ishiguruma*, or Stone Wheel pattern,** becomes the perfect complement when stitched over the traditional Card Tricks block pattern.

Tip

For best results when machine quilting, begin stitching at a pivot point and adjust stitch length so you end exactly at the point, too.

Appliqué "Cousins"

Many sashiko designs strongly resemble traditional American patchwork patterns. **For example, the curved petals of this *Kiku*, or Chrysanthemum pattern, make it a close relative of the classic Dresden Plate design.** Use variations of these and other basic sashiko patterns to provide coordinated quilting designs that will create a feeling of unity throughout a patchwork quilt.

A Sashiko Sampler

Chrysanthemums are but one of many delicately curved, organic designs. **Sashiko flowers bring style, sensibility, and grace to quilts.** Take the sampler approach and create a quilt based on a variety of isolated designs. Working over plain blocks is an ideal way to showcase beautiful designs. Clockwise from upper left are the following flowers: clematis, cherry blossom, wisteria, wood sorrel, and hydrangea (in the center). Enlarge the diagrams on pages 100 and 101 and use them as patterns.

Tip

Mark designs on a light-colored backing fabric and quilt from the back using a heavy thread in the bobbin.

S A S H I K O   S E N S A T I O N S

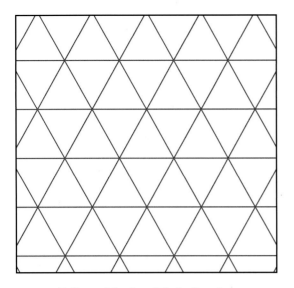

Mitsu-Uroko/Fish Scales

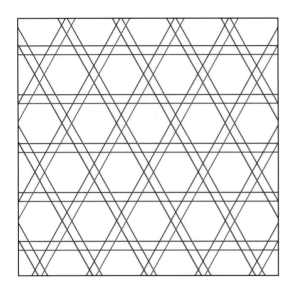

Kagome/Woven Bamboo

Fundo/Counterweights

Sashiko How-To

In these diagrams, the colors suggest an order for stitching. Mark your quilt top in any color that shows up well on your fabrics.

Before stitching, practice on a test piece to determine the best tension. The stitches on the back should look the same as those on the front. As you machine quilt, leave the thread ends long. After machine-stitching the designs, bring thread ends to the back, take a tiny backstitch, run the needle through the batting for a short distance, and then bring it out through the backing. Clip away the thread where it emerges.

For straight-line overall patterns such as the two at the top left of this page, use an acrylic ruler with 60-degree angles to mark your quilt top. For any overall pattern, strive for consistent spacing in a scale that works best for your quilt. To quilt a sashiko design over the entire quilt, refer to the diagrams, and stitch all the lines shown in one color in the following order:

1. ——————
2. ——————
3. ——————
4. ——————
5. ——————
6. ——————

If, however, the sashiko design is confined to an area, try to avoid repeated starts and stops in order to limit the finishing handwork required with thread ends. Strive to keep the pattern continuous, either by pivoting at intersections or stitching-in-the-ditch to move less conspicuously over to the nearest line for sashiko.

For isolated motifs such as those on the opposite page, enlarge each diagram as appropriate. You may wish to trace the full-size pattern onto tissue paper, a tear-away interfacing, or stabilizer. To stitch these continuous-line patterns, start at the center. Stitch along the blue lines first, then proceed, without lifting the presser foot, to the lines shown in red. If necessary, continue on to stitch the green and then orange lines. You will sometimes have a double line of stitching created by two lines of stitching that share the same space or by backtracking over the same line. In each case, you should end where you began.

Tessen/Clematis

Sakura/Cherry Blossom

Ajisai/Hydrangea

Katabami/Wood Sorrel

Fuji/Wisteria

Finish It
Fast

When the clock is ticking and you want to get a quilt finished quickly, you need an easy quilting method that looks great. With all of the simple patterns and designs available today, plus the wide array of decorative threads, ribbons, and buttons now on the market, quick quilting methods are no longer a "make-do" measure. You can still finish your quilts with style in a fraction of the time you might otherwise spend. And that leaves time for making more quilts!

Getting Ready

When getting a quilt finished fast is your goal, choose quilting designs and methods that will fit your time frame. Look for designs that can be stitched freehand, rather than those that require lots of preplanning, measuring, and marking. Consider how the quilt will be used: Quick quilting techniques are perfect for practical quilts like children's and baby quilts or those destined for a college dorm room. And remember, you don't even have to quilt your quilt at all! Tying is a legitimate method of keeping the layers together.

Choose batting that will make whatever type of finishing technique you choose go smoothly and quickly and look great. There are a lot of cotton battings that are needle-punched and hold up well to machine stitching at greater intervals. Most polyester-bonded batts accommodate stitching intervals as much as 4 and 6 inches apart. If you're after a puffy "comforter" look, opt for a high-loft polyester batt.

Quilt It Quick!

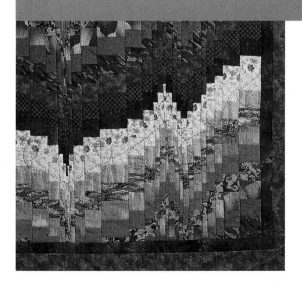

Handwork Where It Counts

Combining basic machine quilting and minimal hand quilting gives you the best of both worlds: The job gets accomplished quickly, but the look proves that you have put your personal mark on your quilt. Begin by machine stitching in the ditch. Then add hand-quilting stitches where they will be most noticeable and appreciated. **Downplay the machine stitching by using clear thread; call attention to the hand quilting by using decorative or contrasting threads.**

Free-Motion, Large-Scale Designs

Large-scale meandering loops, spirals, and swirls can impart a graphic style to a quilt. Think large and bold; enlarge your design by 200 to 400 percent. Let your quilt pattern and fabrics suggest the lines, as **the grapes in the focus fabric of this quilt inspired the loops of grapes and tendrils over the center and the continuous leaf design in the border.** For another look, use a wide zigzag stitch instead of straight stitching; the result can give your quilt the whimsical look of rickrack.

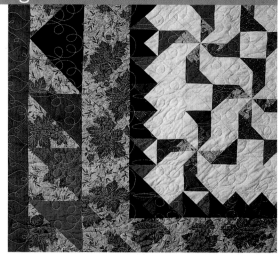

Tacking & Tying

Machine Bar Tacking

Machine bar tacking is extremely fast. Use a wide zigzag and a stitch length near zero. Insert the machine needle 20 times, to create 10 satin stitches that make a square bar tack. **For a hand-tied look, catch a ribbon or yarn bow in each bar tack.** Decorative stitches also make interesting tacking motifs. Straight-stitch or free-motion designs give a quilt an understated elegance. Don't overlook the extra-large decorative designs available on many sewing machines—they make wonderful tacking patterns.

Hand Tying

Hand tying offers many different looks. If you use matching quilting thread, tying is almost invisible from the front of a quilt. To make ties look more prominent, make the knots on the front, using any thread or yarn that will hold tight in a square knot. **Add strands of floss, decorative threads, or yarns to the knots for visual interest. These colorful little fringes can take a quilt from subdued to wonderful.**

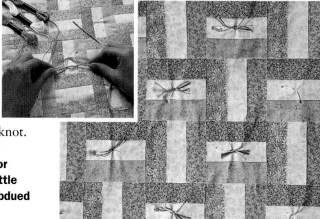

Tip

Help a youngster tie her first quilt so that the project gets completed while the interest is strong.

Buttons

Buttons come in a variety of styles and sizes, from simple to flamboyant. Use buttons at each tie or **position special buttons at focal points of your quilt design.** Use button ties to form designs or patterns, rather than the traditional grid. For a reversible quilt, use buttons on both sides. For hand stitching, choose a button with large holes to accommodate the needle and tie without breaking the bridge between the holes. Consult your sewing machine manual for instructions on attaching buttons by machine.

Do not use buttons on baby or crib quilts. If buttons are pulled loose, they can pose a choking hazard for infants and small children.

Get Help!

Time for a Quilting Bee

Host an old-fashioned quilting bee to speed things up. Invite all your quilting buddies and interested friends. Choose batting that needs minimal quilting. **Space quilting stitches four to an inch, and make use of heavier threads,** such as buttonhole thread, in contrasting colors. **Choose simple, large-scale designs such as spirals and echo quilting.**

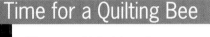

In a group quilting bee, where you can't control the height or tilt of the quilt, you may want to wear a back support of some kind for comfort.

Let Someone Else Quilt It!

The fastest way to finish a quilt may be to let someone else do the quilting with a long-arm commercial quilting machine. But plan ahead; many professional quilters have waiting lists, frequently from 3 to 6 months. To find a qualified and reliable professional quilter, inquire at your local quilt shop or guild, or ask other quiltmakers for their recommendations. **Many professional quilters offer brochures of their designs, so you can choose appropriate quilting patterns for your quilt.**

Some professional quilters will do the layering and basting steps for you, as well as the quilting and binding.

FINISH IT FAST

105

Strategies
from the Experts

It's always interesting and helpful to hear about an expert quilter's approach to choosing quilting designs. To give you as many points of view as possible, we asked 13 quilting experts across the country to talk about their approaches to choosing quilting designs for their quilts. Read on for some valuable insights, ideas, and information you can use whenever you finish a quilt top and wonder, "Now what?"

Hari Walner

Whenever I start to design a quilt, I envision some patchwork and quilting images and a technique that I might want to incorporate. Drawing is more interesting to me than piecing, so I always sketch my quilting designs first and then design the piecing to support them. In Canterbury Tales, I wanted to feature a wreath shape. The wreath design has a lot of movement that would add energy to the quilt, and it looked good with the machine trapunto technique I developed.

Filling in the spaces or shapes of a quilt with compatible quilting designs that fit the main theme is especially fun for me. As this quilt evolved, the wreath seemed to want to have more of a say in the piecing design. That is how the border came about, with the appliquéd edges of the quilted wreaths. That gave the wreath much more of an impact. After I drafted the patchwork, I used the design elements in the wreath as the basis for the quilting designs in the diamonds and corner triangles.

Caryl Bryer Fallert

Feather Study #9
48 × 48 inches

This fantasy feather quilt grew out of a series of hundreds of drawings I did on this theme, all inspired by a close-up view of a feather. I plan my quilt top designs very carefully, but when it comes to the quilting, I like to just respond to the fabric and the design and quilt with patterns that seem fun and interesting. In Feather Study #9, I used many different colors of Madeira Poly-Neon thread to machine quilt, stitching the feather in free-form organic patterns. The ribs of the feather were quilted with parallel lines to echo their arching shapes. I emphasized the circles in the feathers by stitching echoing lines around them several times before swerving off in other directions. The larger areas of the feather are quilted with curving lines that often change directions to correspond to the mottlings of the hand-dyed fabrics and to maintain a sense of movement. I quilted the background with black thread in an overall serpentine meander pattern, to flatten it and make it seem less important.

Robbi Joy Eklow

Queen of Cups
66 × 80 inches

When I am in the right frame of mind, quilting designs simply seem to appear by themselves. As I machine quilt, I'm not really looking at the overall design of the quilt; I only work on what I can see at the time and my face is about 5 inches away from the surface of the quilt. Each area becomes merely a shape that I fill with close quilting. Sometimes I use the countours of an interesting appliqué shape as a guideline for quilting spirals, such as a roll of spirals along the rim of a cup or vase. If I want to simply fill a shape with a quilting pattern, I try to vary the patterns so that the same designs do not occur in adjoining spaces. My approach to quilting also has to do with how I'm feeling that day; sometimes it feels great to stitch long, linear patterns, while on other days it seems more natural to me to be stitching tight spirals. I try to quilt the designs that my subconscious is most comfortable with each day.

Ricky Tims

Songe d'Automne
86 × 86 inches

I have been a quiltmaker for nearly 10 years. I strive to make quilts that have a contemporary look, yet are rooted in tradition. Design, color, and piecing are all aspects of quilting about which I feel confident. Like many quilters, quilting is the part I fear the most, even though I have won many awards. I always wonder if I'm going to ruin an otherwise great quilt by making bad quilting design choices. For Songe d'Automne, I used 100 percent cotton hand-dyed fabrics and chose feathers for the dominant images as a tribute to their historical significance in quilting. I wanted to emphasize the appliquéd motifs in this quilt, so I echoed them with trapuntoed free-form feathers in the dark areas. In the center star points I quilted a free-motion flame pattern. I prefer the look of heavily quilted quilts, so in the remaining background areas I added dense stipple quilting.

110

Marla Hattabaugh

Farther Away
42 × 52 inches

My goal in making quilts is to create art that catches the viewer's attention. Farther Away is one of my African Road series, quilts that I created after returning from a trip to South Africa in 1998. I used one of my favorite quilt motifs, gently curving arrows, on the road, indicating direction, going every which way, crossing over and under each other. I wanted all the arrows to interact and be connected, just as everything in life interacts and connects. I accomplished that with lines of quilting in a thread color that contrasts with most of the fabrics; the quilting provides another form of surface design, making the piece look more complex and interesting. Farther Away is more heavily quilted than most of my quilts, because it seemed to need it in the large, light-colored spaces.

I quilt in a hoop about 99 percent of the time, so I like to plan sections individually. Sometimes I use a Chalkoner to loosely mark a space with quilting lines that I might or might not follow. I spend so many hours with the quilt in my hands and lap, doing the actual quilting, that I am intimately involved with the interaction of the quilt design and the stitching. I love the act of hand quilting, watching the stitched lines develop as they twist and turn throughout the quilt. I also like the freedom of quilting as I go and letting the first lines determine what the next lines will be. As I am finishing the quilting, I check the overall design to make sure that the quilting designs all work together, just as the fabrics do.

Carol Taylor

Falling Leaves
70 × 40 inches

If you find a piece of fabric with wonderful motifs, it can be a great starting point for a quilting design theme. For Falling Leaves, I began with a wonderful leaf print fabric, which I pieced together with a dark hand-dyed fabric. I cut out several white, lacy leaves from the print fabric to fuse to the hand-dyed sections. I like to do mostly free-motion machine quilting, and stitching around and inside those cutouts was the first stage of quilting, to secure them and to add dimension. The real challenge and fun then came from using the sewing machine needle to "draw" leaves on the hand-dyed fabric sections without marking them first. I used 30-weight rayon thread for some of the leaves, and a variegated pearl cotton thread hand-dyed by Melody Johnson and Laura Wasilowski for others. These threads helped lighten and enliven the background areas. My usual style of quilting is to combine a vari-ety of motifs or geometric shapes to fill different sections of a highly pieced top. This quilt, in which I incorporated strictly leaf shapes, is a departure for me, but I am pleased with the results of this self-imposed challenge.

Candy Goff

Joie de Vie
93 × 93 inches

For Joie de Vie, I based the meandering feather plumes on a classic princess feather quilting pattern, which intrigued me with the way it appeared to fold over on itself, creating a sense of movement. (See the detail at upper left on page 106.) To draft the quilting designs, I traced the positive design elements from one quarter of my quilt top onto a piece of tracing paper, outlining the flowers and vases to identify the negative space for quilting. I photocopied the princess feather and its mirror image several times and positioned them in the negative spaces to see where they might fit. I taped them in place, and drew them on another piece of tracing paper, adding the connecting vine and feathers.

Initially, I planned to quilt a ½-inch grid of 60-degree diamonds in the background. However, the ½-inch grid blended into the feathers because there was not enough contrast in the scale. To set off the feathers, I added quilting lines in between, creating a ¼-inch grid. Realizing that this would double the amount of quilting, I considered ways to limit the impact of this decision. I stayed with a ½-inch grid for the 36-inch circle in the center of the quilt, as it did not touch the feathers. And beyond the feathers, I changed from a ¼-inch grid to parallel lines ¼-inch apart, eliminating half of the quilting. This saved some time without sacrificing the sense of balance in the quilting.

From the collection of the Museum of the American Quilter's Society (MAQS), Paducah, KY; photo above and detail on page 106 by Charles R. Lynch, © MAQS.

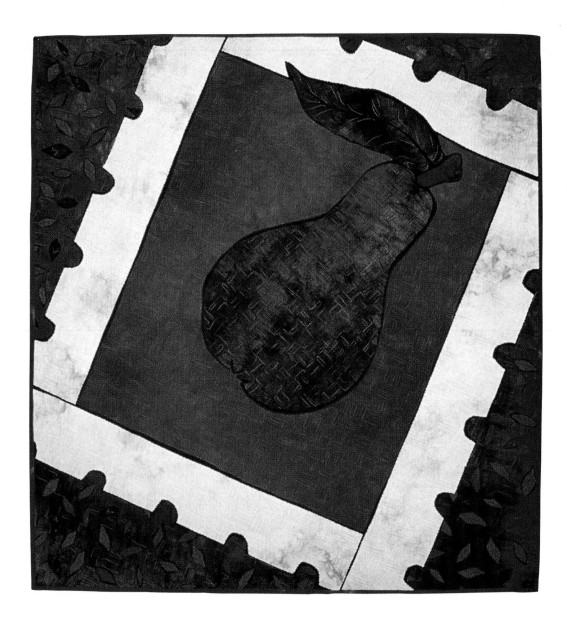

Laura Wasilowski

In order to enhance the simple composition of this quilt, I wanted to use thread that would have a high degree of visibility. I hand-dyed size 12 pearl cotton in colors that would stand out on the fabrics in my quilt and did a simple free-motion quilting design consisting of blocks of parallel lines in a checkerboard pattern. I felt that this direct, simple quilting pattern fit the mood of the quilt perfectly. I liked the alternating blocks of parallel lines and developed variations within that grid. My philosophy of quilting is that the more you do, the better you get, and that quilted designs are more interesting if the thread does not match the background fabric exactly. I think that the rhythm you develop when you quilt is very much like drawing, dancing, or humming a tune. I always start in the middle of a quilt and work my way outward; I try to finish one complete section at a time before taking a break, so that I can keep the tension even within each stitched area.

Melody Johnson

October Harvest
32 × 38 inches

My quilting strategies are based on the design of the quilt; I alternate between believing that the quilting is a completely important design element in the whole quilt design and believing it's merely a supporting structural element. Sometimes I intentionally include large empty spaces in a quilt, which I reserve for fancy quilting, while other times, if the design of the quilt is simply too busy, I do only minimal quilting. Since I teach machine quilting, I stress that each of my students should practice, practice, practice, until she feels "at one" with her sewing machine. When that happens, it's possible to let new ideas for quilting designs pop into your mind and to arrive at your own personal look.

For machine quilting October Harvest, I let the mottlings of my own hand-dyed fabric dictate the areas for separate quilting patterns. I do not mark my quilting designs, since that would take the fun out of quilting for me. However, if there are very large areas of a quilt to cover with quilting designs, I sometimes like to use a soap sliver to mark sections of the piece and focus on those areas individually. As usual, I quilted in contemporary, free-form fans, irregular wavy lines, and stylized feather designs.

Constance Scheele

Where the Grass Grows Tall
83 x 37 inches

For the last several years, my quilts have been inspired by memories of my childhood summers in northwestern Wisconsin. I still try to spend 2 weeks each year near Lake Nebagamon and go canoeing on the Brule River. In my quilt, Where the Grass Grows Tall, I wanted to convey the look of very tall grasses growing from the rocky bottom of a shallow river. I did not want one area or element of the quilt to dominate visually.

As in several other quilts I have hand quilted, I used the long (or seed) stitch, which serves the same function as regular quilting stitches in holding the layers together. However, these longer stitches also provide a totally different visual dimension, an organic, random patterning that mimics textures found in nature. For these stitches, I use a size 10 Hemming between needle and Japanese silk thread by K.N.K. 16, which comes on a card in 20-meter lengths. I cluster these stitches randomly in several areas, always changing the angle from one to the next. The texture these stitches provide adds interest to the back of the quilt, as well as the front.

116

Sue Nickels

Le Panier de Fleurs
67 x 78 inches

My approach to choosing quilting designs for this quilt was to stay true to the style of traditional antique quilts, which I love. This quilt was inspired by a small, sixteenth-century cutwork embroidery piece I saw at the Victoria and Albert Museum in London. I like to do a lot of quilting on my quilts, and by limiting the color and fabric choices in this quilt—a real change from my usual colorful appliqué quilts—I could keep the focus on the quilting. I reinforced the formal and elegant style of this quilt by choosing feathers for the border. I quilted an undulating feather, with the plumes filling the entire border area,

and added small stipple quilting behind the feathers to give them more fullness. The straight-line crosshatching also stays true to the style and look of this quilt. The hardest part was deciding how to quilt the crosshatched lines in the navy area around the basket. I have always quilted straight lines with a walking foot, which is very time consuming and involves a lot of stopping, starting, and repositioning of the quilt. This time, however, I decided to free-motion quilt the crosshatch lines using a darning foot, which worked very well and was a great time-saver, too.

Come Berrying
50 x 50 inches

Jeana Kimball

I put a great deal of thought and time into appliquéing my quilts, and therefore my philosophy and approach to quilting design is that the quilting needs to enhance and complement the appliqué without overpowering it. It is my belief that quilting around appliqué shapes does not necessarily make them puff up, and that quilting on top of appliqué shapes actually adds more dimension. I also think that any background quilting should generally lead the eye to the appliqué motifs.

In Come Berrying, I added dimension by adding veins to the leaves and quilting on top of the berries. (See the detail on page 106 at lower left.) In the background areas of each appliqué block, I stitched diagonal lines radiating outward along all four sides. This creates the illusion of crosshatching without crossing lines, and it's much quicker to stitch. I wanted the quilting to be unobtrusive on the lettering, so I quilted straight lines that follow the grain of the fabric, which makes the quilted lines virtually disappear. For the pieced checkerboard, I eyeballed the intervals to determine the distances between the remaining diagonal straight lines. These decisions helped provide a feeling of overall balance in the design and also maintained the balance of quilting throughout the quilt.

Karen Kay Buckley

Memories of the Holidays
92 x 92 inches

I have done machine quilting as well as hand quilting for many years. I normally quilt my large quilts by hand, and I reserve the smaller projects for machine quilting. However, as I was finishing the extensive appliqué on Memories of the Holidays, I decided—not without some trepidation—to take on the challenge of finishing this rather large quilt with machine quilting. I wanted the quilting to enhance the appliqué designs and not overpower them. The central area is quilted in the ditch, with veins adding detail to each red flower and holly leaf appliqué.

The off-white background is probably where I had the most fun. Using beige thread, I machine quilted holly leaves extending off from the stems of the appliquéd floral motifs. Inside each quilted holly leaf, as with the appliqués, I added veins. (You can see this more clearly in the detail on page 106 at the lower right.) To emphasize the holiday and winter theme, I interspersed simple, double-cross-stitch snowflakes in white thread. Meandering loops that are very close together fill in the rest of the background, including that of the border.

Quilting Designs
Glossary

Adire cloth. A Nigerian fabric of tightly woven cotton in which cassava paste is used as a resist to form patterns when dyeing.

Background quilting. Quilting that fills the area between design elements. Among classic background quilting styles are crosshatching or grids, parallel lines, clamshells, fans, echoes, and stipple quilting.

Button and carpet thread. Heavyweight thread, in cotton and cotton/polyester, used for items where you need a very strong thread. A good choice for places where you want the quilting to stand out and for chunky, folk-style stitches.

Continuous-line design. A quilting design that can be stitched in one long, unbroken line. Continuous designs are especially useful in machine quilting; they eliminate stops and starts, which require you to secure thread ends. In a design such as this, the dot marks the starting and stopping

point, while the arrows indicate stitching direction.

Crosshatch quilting. A straight or diagonal grid of quilting lines that form diamonds or squares in the background of a quilt.

Darning foot. A presser foot with a large opening at its base and a spring mechanism. Used during free-motion quilting, this foot moves up and down with the needle, holding fabric in place when the needle is down, but allowing free motion of the piece when the needle is in the up position.

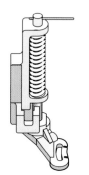

Generic Darning Foot

Echo quilting. Concentric lines of quilting that produce repeating, or echoed, shapes. Echo quilting is most often used around appliqué shapes and quilted motifs. Rows of echo quilting can be spaced equally or by varying amounts.

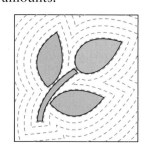

Feathers. Quilting designs that feature teardrop- or comma-shaped plumes along a center vein. Feathered designs can be formed on either side of a straight or wavy line, around a circle for a wreath, or in other arrangements.

120

Feed dogs. A notched mechanism in the throat plate of a sewing machine that grips the bottom layer of fabric. Lowering the feed dogs makes it possible to move fabric through the machine freely for free-motion quilting.

Free-motion quilting. Sewing with the machine's feed dogs disengaged and using a darning foot, so that you can freely move the quilt under the needle, making stitches of any length and in any direction you choose.

Indigo. A deep blue color, formerly derived from a plant. Synthetic indigos have replaced the plant material as a source of blue dye.

Monofilament thread. A very fine (.004 mm) nylon thread most often used through the needle only. Available in clear or smoke, the thread itself is difficult to see in the finished work. Indentations are visible, giving machine-quilted pieces a hand-quilted appearance

Mud cloth. A fabric that is painted with various kinds of iron-rich mud indigenous to Mali, West Africa.

Outline quilting. Outlining a shape with a line of quilting stitches, often placed ¼ inch from the seam.

Pearl cotton. Cordlike thread with a slight sheen, made of loosely twisted cotton fibers (rather than strands, as with embroidery floss). A good choice for larger, bold, folk art quilting stitches, and for tying quilts. Comes in several sizes, from thin (#12 and #8) to thick (#5 and #3). Use with a large-eye embroidery needle.

Sashiko. A Japanese style of quilting, featuring heavyweight white threads and quilting patterns stitched in geometric or curving patterns.

Stencil. A quilting design cut out of medium-weight plastic. Homemade versions may be made from cardboard, and antique versions may be made from tin or another metal. Quilters transfer the design onto a quilt top by drawing with a marking pen or pencil in each slotted opening.

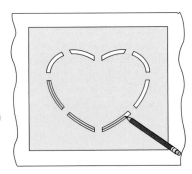

Stipple quilting. Very closely spaced, random lines that resemble pieces of a jigsaw puzzle, generally used to fill in small areas or flatten portions of a quilt in order to emphasize nearby raised motifs. Similar to meander quilting, but stitching lines are much closer together.

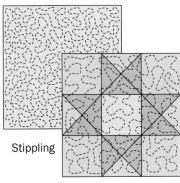

Stippling

Meandering

Stitch-in-the-ditch quilting. Quilting that is done right in the seam of a pieced block or other patchwork.

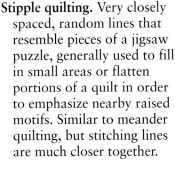

Tacking. Taking several close, zigzag (satin) stitches through the quilt sandwich in one place. Decorative machine stitches can also be used.

Template. A paper, cardboard, or plastic pattern cut in the shape of a quilting design or pattern piece. A marking pen or pencil is used to draw around the template, transferring the design to a quilt top.

Tying. The process of securing the three layers of a quilt sandwich together by tying a knot with sturdy thread, pearl cotton, or yarn.

QUILTING DESIGNS GLOSSARY

Elsie May Campbell grew up with a needle in her hand, participating in 4-H and Make-It-Yourself-with-Wool competitions. Raised in a small Mennonite community in Oklahoma, she learned to quilt at an early age. She began exhibiting quilts in 1992 and has been teaching quiltmaking since 1994. She holds a B.S. in home economics education and a Master's in special education, and she taught in public schools until recently. She is a freelance editor for Chitra Publications and lives in Dodge City, Kansas.

Joe Cunningham has been a quiltmaker, author, and quilt teacher since 1979. His eight books and numerous magazine articles focus on the lessons to be learned from old quilts. His quilts have been shown in exhibitions throughout the United States. He has created a one-man musical show about Joe Hedley, a man who lived in England around 1800 and was known as "Joe the Quilter." Cunningham lives with his wife and two children in San Francisco, where he continues to make quilts, teach quiltmaking, and write about quilts for many publications.

Diane Gaudynski is a self-taught quilt artist who makes traditional quilts using the Harriet Hargrave method for machine quilting. In Waukesha, Wisconsin, where the winters are long and cold, she loves to settle down for serious quiltmaking from January through April of each year. As a teacher and lecturer for 9 years, she loves to encourage beginning quiltmakers. Diane has had seven quilts juried into the AQS show in Paducah, Kentucky, with one winning a second place award, one a first place, and four of her quilts capturing the Bernina Award for Machine Workmanship. She has written magazine articles and has appeared on the PBS documentary *America Quilts*. Diane is a director on the board of Wisconsin Quilters, Inc., and is currently writing a book for AQS about machine quilting.

Myrah Brown Green is a quiltmaker and fashion designer who lives in Brooklyn, New York. Since she began quilting, her quilts have been exhibited in a variety of galleries, museums, and quilt shows. She is a teacher of many quilting techniques and a lecturer on African textiles. She is a member of the Women of Color Quilter's Network and The Quilter's Guild of Brooklyn, New York. One of her quilts appears in *Spirits of the Cloth: Contemporary African American Quilts* and the corresponding traveling exhibit.

Laura Heine won the 1994 Bernina Award for best machine workmanship at the American Quilter's Society Competition in Paducah, Kentucky. She teaches for YLI, and her quilts are featured in their ads and brochures. Laura also designs fabrics for Kings Road Imports; her line of fabric is called "Fondly Flowers." Her two children, Jenna and Brandon, tolerate her quilting obsession and are even beginning to quilt on their own.

Mary Saltsman Parker lives in Asheville, North Carolina. She is the author of *Sashiko: Easy and Elegant Japanese Designs for Decorative Machine Embroidery*. Mary teaches a variety of classes that bring out the creativity that exists in every seamstress. Mary is also chief financial officer for the county school system. Her fondness for cats and her love of sewing have remained strong for years.

Linda Pool lives with her family in Vienna, Virginia. She has been a quiltmaker since 1977 and has taught classes and lectured on quilting techniques since 1982. She was a winner in three of the Great American Quilt Contests sponsored by The Museum of American Folk Art, and was the Virginia State winner in the Memories of Childhood crib quilt contest. Linda has won many other awards and ribbons in major shows around the country, and several of her quilts have been displayed in other countries. Her quilts and articles have appeared in numerous quilting books and magazines. She was a member of the staff of the Jinny Beyer Hilton Head Island Quilting Seminar for 10 years, and she has taught at numerous other quilt shows, festivals, and gatherings. Linda has also served as a judge for several quilt and needlework shows.

Judy Roche has been a quiltmaker since the 1960s and a quilt collector for more than 25 years, specializing in signed and dated Delaware Valley quilts and appliqué quilts. She has always had an interest in social history, and her lectures highlight the importance of quilts in both social and cultural history. Judy has taught beginning quiltmaking and appliqué classes, and she loves collecting fabric. She lives in Solebury, Pennsylvania, with her husband, Patrick, who is a talented folk artist and one of her best critics.

Diane Rode Schneck is a prolific quiltmaker. She calculates that since she has been quilting for over a quarter of a century, it will take her most of this new century to finish quilting all of her unfinished projects. Diane teaches quilting in New York City and at conferences and guilds all across the country. She is known for her scrap quilts and appliqué quilts on a variety of humorous themes. She is co-founder of the popular Phabric Phantom tours, a guided adventure showing quilters and sewers first-hand where to find great fabrics in New York City.

Anita Shackelford is an internationally recognized teacher, lecturer, and author specializing in nineteenth-century dimensional appliqué techniques and original quilting designs. A quiltmaker since 1967, Anita's work has been exhibited across the United States and in Australia, winning many awards, including 12 Best of Show awards. Two of her quilts have received the Mary Krickbaum Award for best hand quilting at a National Quilting Association show. She is the author of *Three-Dimensional Appliqué* and *Embroidery Embellishment Techniques for Today's Album Quilt, Anita Shackelford: Surface Textures, Appliqué with Folded Cutwork,* and *Coxcomb Variations.* She is the designer of several specialty tools, including the Infinite Feathers templates.

Ami Simms has an easygoing teaching style and incorrigible sense of humor that have made her a sought-after instructor on the national circuit for the last 12 years. She was first introduced to quiltmaking in 1975 while conducting research among the Old Order Amish, and she has gone on to make almost 100 quilts. Ami is the creator of the infamous WORST Quilt in the World Contest and the author of eight quilting books, the most recent of which is *Picture Play Quilts.*

Debra Wagner has been a machine quilter for more than 25 years and holds a degree in clothing, textiles, and design. Her main interest is in developing machine methods for traditional quiltmaking. She is a three-time first-place winner at the AQS Show and Contest and a two-time winner of the Bernina Award for Excellence in Machine Workmanship. Her Rail through the Rockies quilt was designated a Masterpiece Quilt by the Master Quilter's Guild Program of the National Quilting Association and was chosen as one of the top 100 quilts of the twentieth century. She has taught internationally, and her work is included in many private and corporate collections.

Acknowledgments

We gratefully thank the many people and companies who have generously contributed to this book.

Quiltmakers, Samplemakers, and Quilt Collectors

Nancy Bishoff, Summer Sherbet baby quilt, 2000, quilted by Linda Carey, on page 12

Karen Kay Buckley, Memories of the Holidays, 2000, on page 119 and detail on page 106

Elsie May Campbell, Apples, 2000, on pages 14 and 15; Art Nouveau Quilt, 2000, on page 19; Bow-Ties, 1995, on page 12; Great Grandma Goebel's Red & Green Appliqué Quilt, 1993, details on cover and on page 12; Let Freedom Ring, 1994, on page 45, courtesy of Mary Korte; Pastel Quilt top on pages 10, 11, and 15; Pharoah's Phans, 1996, on pages 16 and 17; Sweethearts, 1996, on page 14

Mary Clark, Lone Star, 1993, on page 76

Marie Colello, Free Spirit, 1999, details on pages 102 and 103, courtesy of Kristine Colello

Margaret Dunsmore, Dancing in the Rain, 1998, detail on page 83, photo by Roger Bird

Robbi Joy Eklow, Queen of Cups, 2000, on page 109, photos by the artist

Caryl Bryer Fallert, Feather Study #9, 1999, on page 108 and details on pages 19 and 108, photos by the artist

Diane Gaudynski, October Morning, 1999, on page 22 and details on pages 23 and 24, collection of the Museum of the American Quilter's Society (MAQS), Paducah, KY, photo by Richard Walker, © MAQS; Sixteen Baskets of Mud, 1997, on pages 2–3 and 24; Rose of Sharon, 1999, on page 25; Wholecloth Mini, 2000, on page 25

Felicia Geiter, Purple Delight, 1999, on pages 102 and 104, quilting by Jacklyn Hazen/Sister's Choice

Candy Goff, Joie de Vie, 1998, on page 113 and detail on page 106; collection of the Museum of the American Quilter's Society (MAQS), Paducah, KY, photos by Charles R. Lynch, © MAQS

Elaine Gottshall, Star Cats, 2000, on page 105

Myrah Brown Green, Sankofa, 2000, on page 90

Marla Hattabaugh, Farther Away, 2000, on page 111, photos by the artist

Laura Heine, Machine Quilting Sampler, 2000, on pages 64 and 68 using the Painted Petals fabric collection she designed for King's Road Imports

Eleanor Hickman, Country Morning, 1996, page 80; Clematis, 1997, page 81; Potting Shed, 1999, page 82; Peaceful Valley, 1997, page 82; Veggies 'Good for You,' 1998, page 83; photos by Judy Mercer Tescher

Melody Johnson, October Harvest, 1997, on page 115, photos by the artist

Jeana Kimball, Come Berrying, 1994, on page 118 and detail on page 106

Corienne L. Kramer, 1830s-style medallion quilt top, on page 61; Pinwheel, 1999, on page 105

Eleanor Levie, For Max, 2000, on page 60 and detail on page 63

Sue Nickels, Le Panier de Fleurs, 2000, on page 117, photo by Sue Holdaway-Heys

Ellen Pahl, Simple Shapes #4, 2000, with fabrics from Maywood Studios, on pages 52, 54, and 55

Mary Saltsman Parker, Chrysanthemum Basket, 2000, on page 96

Linda Pool, Floral Wreath Quilt, 2000, on pages 36–41

Judy Roche, Variable Star, 2000, on pages 30–35, piecing by Corienne L. Kramer, quilting by Toby Preston of Kindred Spirits

Constance Scheele, Where the Grass Grows Tall, 1999, on page 116, photo by the artist

Diane Rode Schneck, Just Desserts, 2000, on page 84 and detail on page 86; Earth and All Stars!, 1993, on page 105; A Cup of Tea with my Quilting Friends, 1992, on page 86

Anita Shackelford, Double Nine Patch, 1984, on page 75; Amish Center Diamond, 1985, on page 72, and details on pages 74 and 77; Broderie Perse Vase of Flowers, 1984, on page 77; Feather Sampler, 2000, on page 75; Feathered Heart Wall Quilt, 2000, on pages 75 and 76

Ami Simms, In & Out the Window, on page 62; Sweet Dreams, on page 63; Dots & Boxes, on page 62; Stepping Stones, on page 62; Bee's Garden, on page 61; all 1999–2000

Carol Taylor, Falling Leaves, 1997, on page 112, photos by the artist

Ricky Tims, Songe d'Automne, 2000, on page 110 and detail on page 106, photo by Van Zandbergen Photography

Eija Vesterqvist, Summer Window, 1996, on page 87

Hari Walner, Canterbury Tales, 1999, on pages 4–5 and 107, photo by Brian Birlauf, as featured in *Exploring Machine Trapunto: New Dimensions* (C&T Publishing Co., 1999)

Laura Wasilowski, Via Pear Mail, 2000, on page 114, photos by the artist

Joelene A. Weaver and Heather Salasky, Tied Rail Fence Baby Quilt, 2000, on page 104

Additional samples and quilt tops were made by Cyndi Hershey, Corienne L. Kramer, and Eleanor Levie. Nineteenth-century quilts on pages 46–50 are from the collections of Judy Roche and Corienne L. Kramer.

Original Pattern Designs

Diane Gaudynski, feathered designs and urn on pages 28 and 29; **Myrah Brown Green,** pages 94–95; **Laura Heine,** pages 70–71; **Jeana Kimball,** hare pattern on page 29, reprinted with her permission from her quilt, Fairmeadow and pattern book, also titled *Fairmeadow,* from Foxglove Cottage (see "Resources" on page 126); **Diane Rode Schneck,** pages 88 and 89; **Anita Shackelford,** pages 78 and 79; **Eija Vesterqvist,** page 89.

Sashiko patterns are from **Mary Saltsman Parker;** other designs appear in her book, *Sashiko* (Lark Books, 1999).

Fabrics and Supplies

American & Efird, Inc.—Mettler threads, Signature machine quilting threads

Sonya Lee Barrington—hand-dyed fabrics used in the quilt top on pages 30–35

Benartex—fabrics

Bernina of America—Virtuosa 150 sewing machine

Fiskars—embroidery scissors, rotary cutters

Maywood Studios, a division of E. E. Schenck—fabrics for Simple Shapes #4 on pages 52, 54, and 55

Olfa—rotary cutters

Omnigrid—acrylic rulers, cutting mats

P & B Textiles—fabrics

Quilter's Rule International—quilt stencils

Rowenta—Professional iron

The carved wall box and painted Pennsylvania German miniature blanket chest on page 42 were made by Pat Roche of Solebury, Pennsylvania. Thanks to Materese Roche for the use of her steamer, to Judy Roche for lending us her metal stencils, and to the Martin Brooks Nursery for freshly cut bamboo shown on page 96. The card on page 43 is reproduced by permission from the American Greetings Corporation, © AGC, Inc.

Sonya Lee Barrington
837 47th Avenue
San Francisco, CA 94121
(415) 221-6510
E-mail: slbstudio@jps.net
Bundles of hand-dyed fabrics

Beautiful Publications, LLC
7508 Paul Place
Loveland, CO 80537
(970) 622-9950
Continuous-line patterns for machine quilting

Clotilde, Inc.
B3000
Louisiana, MO 63353-3000
(800) 772-2891
General quiltmaking supplies

EQuilter.com
African, Egyptian, and tribal theme fabrics

Fiberworks
1310 24th Street W
Billings, MT 59102
(406) 656-6663
Web site:
    www.fiberworks-
    heine.com
Fabrics, machine-quilting threads, general quilt-making supplies

Foxglove Cottage
P.O. Box 18297
Salt Lake City, UT 84118
Fairmeadow quilt pattern book

International Fabric Collection
3445 West Lake Road
Erie, PA 16505
(814) 838-0740
Web site: www.intfab.com
Fabrics from around the world, including Africa

Ola Trading Co.
6030 Highway 85, Suite 238
Riverdale, GA 30274
(770) 996-3106
Web site:
    www.AfricanFabrics.com
African fabrics

Primrose Gradations
P.O. Box 6
Two Harbors, MN 55616
(218) 525-0619
Web site: www.dyearts.com
Hand-dyed fabrics

Quilter's Rule International, LLC
817 Mohr Avenue
Waterford, WI 53185
(800) 343-8671 or
    (262) 514-2000
Web site:
    www.quiltersrule.com
Quilting stencils

Roxanne Products Company
742 Granite Avenue
Lathrop, CA 95330
(800) 993-4445
Web site:
    www.thatperfectstitch.com
Hand quilting needles

The Stencil Company
28 Castlewood Drive
Cheektowaga, NY 14227
(716) 656-9430
E-mail: stencil@webt.com
Quilting stencils

StenSource International, Inc.
18971 Hass Avenue
Sonora, CA 95370
(209) 536-1148
E-mail:
    generalinfo@stensource.com
Quilting stencils

EZ Quilting by Wrights
85 South Street
P.O. Box 398
West Warren, MA 01092-0398
Stitchable Stencils by Hari Walner, laser-cut paper stencils for machine quilting

Thimble Works
P.O. Box 462
Bucyrus, OH 44820
Web site:
    www.thimbleworks.com
Infinite Feathers Design Template

YLI Corporation
161 West Main Street
Rock Hill, SC 29730
(800) 296-8139
E-mail: ylicorp@ylicorp.com
Web site: www.ylicorp.com
YLI Jeans Stitch, 100 percent cotton quilting thread, Colors by YLI variegated quilting thread, machine quilting thread, and decorative threads

Index

INDEX

Quilting Styles

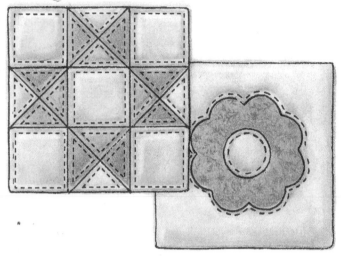

Outline Quilting

Echo Quilting

Single

Double

Crosshatch or Grid Quilting

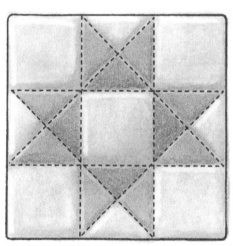

In the Ditch Quilting

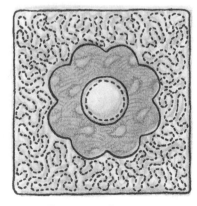

Stipple Quilting

Meander Quilting